WORKING WITH COLOUR

 a beginn

PAULINE WILLS

Photographic credits

David Parker/Science Photo Library: Plate 1; Manley Palmer Hall, Philosophical Research Society, taken from a painting by Mihran K. Serailian (USA) titled *The Seven Spinal Chakras*, previously reproduced in *Subtle Body* by David V. Tansley published by Thames and Hudson, 1994: Plate 4; Jean Claude Ciancimino (London), previously reproduced in *Tantra* by Philip Rawson published by Thames and Hudson, 1993: Plate 5; R. Sheridan/Ancient Art and Architecture Collection: Plate 6; John Glover/Garden Picture Library: Plate 7; M.A. Mackenzie/Robert Harding Picture Library: Plate 8.

A catalogue record for this title is available from the British Library.

ISBN 0 340 670118

First published 1997
Impression number 10 9 8   7 6   5 4   3 2   1
Year   2000   1999   1998   1997

Typeset by Transet Limited, Coventry, England.
Printed in Great Britain for Hodder & Stoughton Educational, a division of Hodder Headline plc, 338 Euston Road, London NW1 3BH by Cox and Wyman Limited, Reading, Berks.

CONTENTS

Chapter 3   The colours of the spectrum   24

Chapter 4   Our own aura of colour 37

Chapter 5   Using colour for self-help   58

INTRODUCTION

Colour is a wonderful phenomenon which constantly surrounds us. We find it displayed in nature through the variative colours of flowers, foliage and trees which, with the passing of the seasons, change from spring green, to dark green and then to reds, oranges, yellows and browns of autumn. It is found in the plumage of birds, exhibited to its fullness by the male bird during courtship. We experience the translucent colours of gem stones which grow in the darkness of the earth and manifest their energy of light when mined and brought to the surface.

We also witness the wonder of colour through the incredible display of polar lights, known as the aurora borealis, and in the rainbow which spreads across the sky when the sun appears after a storm. To the Norse people, the rainbow was the bridge by which heroes who died in battle crossed to their reward in Valhalla, the place of bliss for the souls of slain heroes; the Greeks saw it as Iris, the messenger of the gods, and the Greenlanders said it was the hem of God's cloak.

Stand still for a moment and look around you. Observe the myriad of colours interwoven in your surrounding space and in the clothes that you are wearing. If you are reading this in your own home, think about why you selected the colour scheme of your room. Was it because the colours are your favourites, or because they have a specific physical or psychological effect upon you. You might also ask the same question about the colour of the clothes that you are wearing. Each colour, because it vibrates to a set frequency, has a marked effect upon us: illuminatory colour more so than pigment colour. A great deal of information can be gleaned about a person by the colours they wear.

People who work with colour, namely artists, designers and colour

practitioners, become sensitive to the vibrational energies of colour. This enables them to select the colour or colours which will benefit them physically, emotionally, mentally and spiritually. Once selected, there are many ways that these colours can be worked with.

We as humans are beings of light. We are surrounded and interpenetrated by a constantly changing rainbow of light, known as the aura. The colour, or lack of colour, reflects our health patterns and moods. I believe that the physical body is only a vehicle through which our feelings and thoughts manifest. Disease starts in the aura, and if not eradicated at this level, will manifest in the physical body. How true the saying: 'I feel off colour'. If we believe that we are beings of light, should we not also believe that we can be healed with the vibrational frequencies of colour which constitute light. I believe that we can and that vibrational medicine, encompassing both light and sound, will become the medicine of the future.

The aim of this book is to bring greater awareness and understanding of colour to all those who feel drawn towards, or wish to know more about its vibrational energies. It also describes the many ways in which these energies can be used.

This book will explore how colour is used in nature and its symbolic significances in various cultures and tribes. It will aim towards teaching colour sensitivity and the qualities pertaining to each colour; how colour manifests and the differentiation between pigment and illuminatory colour. It will also examine the electromagnetic field or aura which surrounds all living things. Ideas will be given for the beneficial use of colour in the home, garden and in clothing.

Practical work is given throughout the book to aid your appreciation of colour so that you may learn how to use the beneficial qualities pertaining to the colour spectrum.

I have been working with colour for approximately fifteen years. I first became attracted to it through the study of yoga. I read all I could find on the subject and then trained to become a colour practitioner. Since working with colour therapeutically, and in conjunction with yoga and reflexology, I have seen and experienced the wonderful results that it can procure. Try to visualise what a dull, uninteresting world it would be without colour.

COLOUR THROUGHOUT THE WORLD

Colour is an immediate experience, acting directly on the emotions, and yet it is curiously abstract. It affects us physically, psychologically, mentally, emotionally and spiritually, and has been expressed in religious symbolism throughout the ages.

As far as we know, colour has existed since the beginning of time. It has been utilised by both the plant kingdom and the animal kingdom. It has been used to express fear, danger, joy, death, birth and puberty. It has been used to appease the gods and as a form of protection.

The plant world

Colour is a gift of evolution which has been exploited by the plant world for its survival. Flowers have evolved to produce the colours that will attract only the insects most suited to spreading their pollen for fertilisation. The white flowers of the yucca plant attract a night-flying moth which collects and transports the pollen grains from the bloom.

The carotenoid pigments of red, orange and yellow, which colour the petals of flowers such as tulips, dandelions and chrysanthemums, act as a sunscreen to protect the delicate plant tissue from damage by atmospheric radiation. The flowers and vegetables in the blue–red colour range, such as blackberries, red cabbage, roses and geraniums, gain their colour from anthocyanins. These are

substances which act as natural indicators of change in the acidity of the cell sap in which they are dissolved. It is therefore possible that these protect the plant from the effects of mineral deficiency as well as from high levels of radiation.

The animal world

The colours of animals may also be the result of nature's way of ensuring the survival of the fittest. The colour vision which each species possesses has evolved for detecting food and for finding and recognising each other. The role an animal's colour plays in its search for food can be illustrated by the Borneo crab spider. This creature is shaped and coloured to look like white bird droppings; it preys on insects that feed on real bird droppings.

The colours displayed by animals are also used to attract members of the opposite sex and for camouflage. Animals that live in snowy regions tend to be coloured white; those that live in the forest may be green or brown.

Most poisonous insects and animals are brightly coloured with sharply contrasting patterns. This warns likely predators to leave well alone. There are creatures which are able to 'mimic' and use the colouring of poisonous species as a form of protection.

Early tribal communities

Travelling back to the early human communities, we find that colour was used for body painting and in their rituals. The more one investigates the symbolism of the colours used by the various tribes in different regions of the world, the more one realises that no absolute meanings can be attributed to these colours. The colours most extensively used were red, black and white, most probably because these colours were easily accessible. Red was obtained from ochre, a native pigment composed of fine clay and an iron oxide; black was

4

taken from the soil and from charcoal, and white was derived from clay.

The symbolism of these colours changed according to the ritual context. White, as semen, signified male generative power; as milk, it was a feminine symbol used at a girl's initiation ceremonies; as water, it was connected with spiritual purity. The red of blood was synonymous with power, which can be used for good or ill. Red ochre, when scattered on a grave or painted on a corpse, was symbolic of renewal; of life after death. Black signified death and mourning. It was used in circumcision rites to signify the death of a child to the status of adult.

The simplest use of self decoration among tribal communities was a form of identification. Certain patterns and colours enabled members of the same tribe to identify each other. Colour was similarly used at important stages of a person's life, namely pregnancy, birth, puberty, marriage and death.

On special occasions, a whole community would adhere to a chosen colour. Fertility rites would encompass black to attract the dark, rain-bearing clouds to promote fertility. In some tribes, the men would use black against the 'Evil Eye'. They believed that adorning themselves with this colour made them appear more frightening. In times of war, men would adorn themselves with grey leaves and charcoal. In some tribes, when a member died, the women covered themselves in white clay as a sign of mourning. The reason for this could lie in the fact that they associated white with spirits, the spirits of their ancestors.

As a member of a tribe journeyed into old age, body decoration ceased. Instead, a simple form of clothing was worn. The body was no longer looked upon as a thing of beauty, therefore it had to be covered.

Colour was and still is associated with alchemy, an early form of chemistry which originated in Alexandria about AD 100 and survived for fifteen centuries before giving way to modern science. The alchemists believed that base metals, such as lead and iron, could be changed into gold. Gold was looked upon as the essence of the sun, the equilibrium of all metallic properties. The esoteric meaning of turning base metal into gold is the transmutation of the soul.

Medieval times

Carl Gustav Jung (1875–1961), a Swiss psychologist, found himself drawn to exploring medieval alchemy in order to try to discover the meaning of the constant recurrence of certain symbols and colours in the dreams and paintings of his patients. In 1930, he chanced upon some old alchemical texts which showed the vital role that colour played in this science. It explained that the different hues, which appeared as the alchemist transmuted substances in his vessel, were symbolic of each stage of the inner transformation that he was undergoing. They called this process magnum opus, meaning 'Great Work'. When Jung compared the colours and symbols which appeared in his patient's dreams with the colours and symbols which described alchemical composition, he realised that they were the same. The basic colours which alchemists used were green, black, white, red and gold.

Green was depicted in the lion or dragon, representing the beginning of the Great Work which was the preparation for their science. The first stage of the Great Work was likened to black which contains no colour. The second stage was imbued with the colour white, representing quicksilver, the moon and the feminine principle, and the purity of undivided light. Red was the colour attributed to the third stage. This colour represented the masculine principle, the sun and sulphur. Gold was thought to be the zenith point of colour.

During the Middle Ages, many of the alchemical symbols and colours were adapted for use by the Christian Church. This establishment divided human life into four main stages; baptism, confirmation, marriage and death. The rituals celebrating these stages took place amidst the dancing hues of stained glass and icons.

The wonderful array of colour portrayed in stained glass windows goes back as far as the sixth century. The purpose of these windows in churches was two-fold. First, in an age of almost total illiteracy, the biblical stories depicted in the glowing colours of the glass could be understood. Second, stained glass was purported to radiate the light to illuminate people's minds. It was hoped that the congregation would travel through this light in order to comprehend the greater light of God.

The Religious World

The Christian Church

The colours adopted by the Christian Church have their own language, and the colours of the vestments worn by the priest officiating at a ceremony are symbolic of the occasion.

Christianity associates black with evil and hell. One of the names given to Satan is the 'Prince of Darkness'. Black is the colour of mourning and the colour worn by a priest at a requiem mass.

Red is the colour worn by priests at Whitsuntide and for the feast days of martyrs because it symbolises the fire of Pentecost and Christ's Passion. The red hats of the Pope's cardinals were a reminder that their job was to defend the Church even to the point of shedding blood.

Yellow is linked with sacredness and divinity and is the colour used on the feast days of confessors.

The colour identified with immortality, hope and the growth of the Holy Spirit in humans is vernal green. In medieval times, this colour became associated with the seasons of Trinity and Epiphany in the Church's calendar. Green symbolised the birth of a new year, signifying God's provision for human needs.

To the 'Great Mother', known in many religions as the 'Queen of Heaven', is given the colour blue. It is the colour associated with the Virgin Mary, the mother of Christ. Christians relate this colour to heavenly truth and eternity.

In medieval times, purple was regarded as the most sacred colour. The reason for this could have been its scarcity and high cost. Purple is derived from red and blue. Blue represented spirit and red blood. For this reason it was, and still is, used at passiontide to represent the penance of the individual sinner and the sufferings of Christ. It was also the colour denoting priestly rule and authority.

7

Gold is a colour much used in religious art. One of its uses is to depict the halos around the heads of saints and enlightened beings. This colour also represents God as uncreated light and divine power.

White is the colour of illumination, purity and innocence. It is the colour used for saints who have not been martyred, and at the great festivals of Easter, Christmas, Epiphany and Ascension.

Grey and brown are colours employed to portray the renunciation of the body in order to gain immortality of the soul. This is the reason why the habits of certain religious communities are made in these colours.

Buddhism

Buddhism, one of the great world religions, originated in India, from where it spread to other parts of Asia. This religion likewise applies colour in symbolism. It regards black as the darkness of bondage, whereas brown it relates to the earth. Red is attributed to life, creativity and activity. The colour orange is related to love and happiness. This is reflected in the blessed fruit of the 'fingered citron'. This fruit is purported to resemble the shape of the Buddha's hand. Blue empathises peace and tranquillity.

One of colours which Buddhists hold to be very sacred is yellow. Statues and photographs of the Buddha frequently show him wearing a yellow robe. The saffron robes worn by Buddhist monks symbolise renunciation, desirelessness and humility. The other sacred colour is gold. Gold signifies God as uncreated light and divine power. This colour has a close affiliation with white. White stands for pure consciousness and illumination, a state which is desired if one is to experience and become one with the light and power of the ultimate reality, namely God.

According to Buddhist theory, the colour affiliated with life is vernal green, but the colour attributed to death is pale green. Black, the complementary colour of white, is related to the darkness of bondage. Blue is recognised as a cold colour and associated with the coolness of the heavens and the seas.

Hinduism

The attributes afforded to some of the colours used in Buddhism are the same as those used in Hinduism. The colours which differ are black, blue, gold and white.

The colour black is aligned with the lowest state of being known as *tamas*. This state encompasses lethargy and sensuality. White is associated with the third and highest state *sattva* representing peace and divine truth.

For the Hindu, gold means immortality, light and truth. Gold is associated with Agni, the Hindu god of fire and one of the three great deities. Another god with which Hindus associate colour is Indra. Indra is the ruler of heaven and is always depicted wearing a coat of blue.

Judaism

The colours used in the Jewish religion are mainly taken from the Hebrew qabalistic tree of God. This tree symbolises all creation and is said to grow in the middle of the Holy City.

The colour black stands for understanding and for the kingdom; blue is for mercy; green for victory; grey for wisdom; orange for splendour; red for severity; violet for the foundation; white for joy and cleansing; yellow for beauty.

Amerindans

The Amerindans, the name given to the native inhabitants of the American continent, were also known as the 'red men' or 'red skins'. They worshipped spirits who they believed watched over the tribe and its possessions. They could paint well and used paint to adorn their bodies.

For them, black represented the north, mourning and night. Blue depicted the sky and stood for peace. The colour red portrayed joy,

9

fertility and the red of the day as opposed to the black of the night. Sacredness was displayed in white and yellow and was the colour which described the setting sun.

ANCIENT RELIGIONS

Medieval followers of paganism believed that the world was created from four basic elements. To each of these elements a colour was ascribed. Earth was identified with black; Water with white; Fire with red; Air with yellow. The physical body was viewed as a microcosm of the macrocosm and the elements in the physical body took the form of bodily fluids. Thus earth and black was linked with bile; water and white was phlegm; fire and red was blood; air and yellow was yellow bile.

The seasons and stages of Life

Colour was linked to the rites connected with the four seasons in the Middle Ages. To the peasants, farming was an important and established way of life. The food which the seasons provided gave nourishment and sustenance. For these people, black represented the earth as the sacred womb which nourished the seedlings prior to their birth in the spring. Green heralded the spring and new life, and brown was identified with decay, rest and preparation for a new cycle to begin.

The seasons were associated with specific gods and goddesses in ancient Greece and these were vested with the appropriate colour. Spring belonged to Artemis and the colour yellow; summer was attributed to Athena and the colour white; black represented winter and linked with the infernal gods of the underworld; autumn was given to Dionysus, the god of wine, and to the colour red.

The four seasons, with their corresponding colours, frequently symbolised the four stages of life. Birth was generally associated with white. Pregnant women in the Trobriand Islands are shaded with special mantles to keep them in the 'white condition', believed to promote softness and fertility. White also relates to puberty. West African boys are daubed with this colour to represent either the white spirits of their ancestors or the white semen of their dawning maturity. White, too, is the colour of marriage. In this context it signifies not only purity but the change that will take place as the bride enters this phase of her life. She is leaving her parents to start a new life with her husband. A Hindu bride wears a yellow gown to echo the fruitfulness of the harvest. In some countries, it is customary for the wedding guests to wear red for love, sex and joy.

The end of the earthly life and the transition to the next is connected to a variety of colours, depending on the country and its traditions. In Europe, black is used for death and widows dress themselves in 'widow's weeds'. In China and other Eastern countries, the colour for mourning is white. This is symbolic of many things. It stands for the status of the soul which has moved from its earthly to its spiritual home. The colour of undyed cloth is white, signifying sorrow and humility in some cultures. In places like Bali and the West Indies, where it is believed that the soul transgresses to a much better place, bright and cheerful colours are worn to celebrate this transition.

The planets

In medieval times, the seven colours were aligned to the planets and to each of these was designated a gem stone and a metal. Yellow/gold belonged to the sun and was affiliated to gold and topaz; silver/white was allocated to the moon with silver and pearl; red was given to Mars with iron and ruby; purple encompassed Mercury, quicksilver and amethyst; blue pertained to Jupiter, tin and sapphire; green was related to Venus, copper and emerald; black belonged to Saturn alongside lead and diamond.

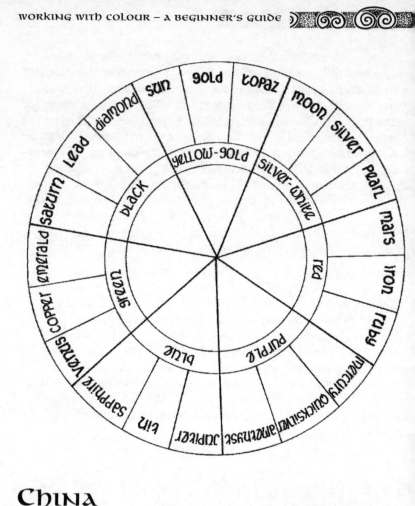

China

China, a country which is reputed to have an alchemical tradition that is older than Europe's, encompasses five elements in their system of healing, namely acupuncture. Acupuncture, which has its roots in classical Chinese medicine, teaches that the vital force, *chi*, circulates in the body through meridians. These meridians, which are bilateral, are either 'yin' or 'yang', depending upon which way *chi* flows. Each meridian has an inner and outer branch. The inner branch passes through one of the major organs of the physical body after which the meridian is named. The Chinese believed that physiological functions were based on the humoral system which encompassed the five elements. As well as working with the yin and yang aspect of the meridians, traditional Chinese acupuncture included working with these elements and their attributes, one of which was colour.

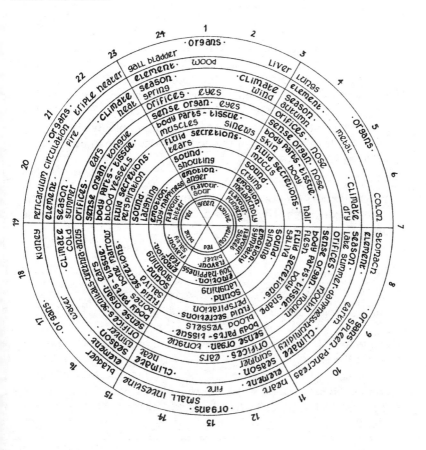

They related Earth to yellow; Air (metal) to white; Water to blue; Wood (ether) to green; Fire to red. They believed that the ideal time to treat a meridian was when it reached its potential *chi*. This happened for two out of every twenty-four hours.

The way in which colour has been and is used, and its power, are limitless. It affects and manipulates us in all walks of life. Johann Wolfgang Goethe, the author of *Farbenlehre*, thought that the effects of colour are immediately associated with the emotions. He thought of red and yellow as 'plus' colours because they incited lively feelings and excitability. His 'minus' colours were blue, green and blueish-red. These he described as giving a restless, anxious impression.

For most people, the colours at the heat end of the spectrum, namely red, orange and yellow, are cheerful, stimulating provocative and arousing. Those colours at the cool end of the spectrum, encompassing turquoise, blue and violet, create expansion and an air of mysticism, peace and melancholy. The colour which lies between these two bands is green. In some people this colour evokes the tranquil peace of the countryside, while in others it draws nausea.

All of us can make colour serve us by exploring the impact of different colours on our psyche and by taking time to experiment with and learn the many shades of colour which constitute visible light.

PRACTICE

For this simple exercise and for other exercises in this book, you will need a set of coloured crayons or pencils. Colour the two diagrams in this chapter with the colours marked. You can either colour the inner circle where the names of the colours are printed or you can colour the complete circle. If you choose to colour the complete circle, make the colours in the inner circle dense and then gradually fade the colours to a pale shade as you reach the outer circle.

THE MANIFESTATION
OF COLOUR

In the beginning was the sacred darkness,
Out of which came the light,
The light and darkness danced the dance of creation,
And the colours of the spectrum were born.

Theo Gimbel

On every waking moment of our life, colour affects us emotionally, physically, mentally and psychologically, and when we sleep it penetrates our dreams. But for all this, it is generally taken for granted and unstudied by the majority of people. One of its most spectacular appearances is the rainbow.

For centuries it was a mystery as to the cause of the vivid bands of colour which appeared across the sky after a storm, and the reasons why the colours always appeared in the same order. From the time of the Greek philosopher Aristotle, philosophers tried to explain this phenomenon. They believed that the colours were the result of the differing mixtures of light and darkness. They stated that the purest and most brilliant light was white light which, when mixed with a little darkness or 'shadow', produced red. If a greater proportion of darkness was present, the result would be the emergence of green. They believed that blue was the nearest colour to black, therefore to produce this colour, a lot of 'shadow' had to be present.

The colour spectrum

The truth of how the colour spectrum is produced was accidentally discovered by Sir Issac Newton in 1665. While investigating something entirely different, Newton discovered that when he passed sunlight through a prism, the light was refracted, thereby producing the colour spectrum. He suspected that the colours produced by the prism must be mixed together in white light to begin with and that they become visible only because each colour has a different angle of refraction. He tested this theory by placing a second inverted prism in the path of the spectrum formed by the first. The inverted prism caused the colours to recombine into white light.

Through his experiment, he concluded that light is composed of a number of waves, each having a different wavelength and frequency. When these waves penetrate a prism, each one is refracted at a different angle. He observed that red light, with the longest wavelength and lowest frequency, has the smallest angle of refraction; violet light with the shortest wavelength and highest frequency has the largest angle of refraction.

A rainbow is created when the sun's rays are refracted through droplets of rain. Normally a rainbow appears as a single arc, but if the raindrops are large enough for some of the sunlight to be reflected twice inside the raindrop, a second rainbow will appear. This second rainbow will appear above the first but its colours are always fainter and in reverse order. It is also recognised that the larger the drops of rain, the purer and brighter the appearance of the refracted colours.

Nature contains no real colours. It contains only the numerous wavelengths which constitute light. These wavelengths are absorbed and reflected by all objects which surround it. The wavelengths which are reflected enter our eyes and hit the inner lining of the eye, the retina, which contains rods and cone cells. There are three types of cone cells which are responsible for colour vision in daylight and are sensitive to the red, blue and green wavelengths. The rods take over as the light starts to fade into night and these cells are thought

to be more sensitive to blue/green light. They also have the ability to distinguish clearly between the light and shade. When the light hits the retina, the rod and cone cells transmit the signals that light triggers, via the optic nerve, to the visual centre at the back of the brain. It is only when this has occurred that we 'see' colour. To see white light, the wavelengths of all the colours have to hit the retina at the same moment.

The quantum theory

The colours displayed through nature, in the clothes which we wear and in decoration, could not exist without the energy of light. This was not fully understood until the development of the quantum theory.

This theory was originated in 1887 by the physicist Philipp Lenard. He discovered that certain metals emit electrons. When these electrons absorb light, an electric current flows. At the time of his discovery, the knowledge pertaining to the properties of light could not explain this supposition. It was not until 1900 that a German physicist, Max Planck, put forward the theory that energy can only be released or absorbed in packets or quanta. Energy constitutes many forms and is derived from the atom. Atoms constitute a positively charged nucleus which is orbited by negatively charged electrons. The positive charge of the nucleus is balanced by the negative charge of the orbiting electrons.

It was Albert Einstein, a German Swiss physicist, who proved that light is composed of small packets of energy or quanta. These quanta he called photons. In light, a quanta constitutes the smallest amount of light in any given wavelength which can interact with matter.

The colours of the spectrum, with their many hues, are composed of photons. The longer the wavelength, the more spaced-out the photons. In the colours blue, indigo and violet, the wavelengths are short with compacted photons, therefore these colours possess the most energy. The colours at the other end of the light spectrum, namely red, orange and yellow, possess long wavelengths and

therefore less energy. When light falls on an object, some of the photons are absorbed, some transmitted and some reflected. The photons which are absorbed have to have enough vibration to interact with the electrons orbiting within the atomic shells of the object. The electrons, after absorbing the photons' minute quantity of energy, rise to a higher frequency where the absorbed energy is then released as an unmeasurably small amount of heat. The photons which are not of a high enough vibration to excite the electrons are reflected and seen by the eye as colour.

All matter has the ability to absorb and reflect different degrees of light, but pigment compounds are the most efficient agents of selective absorption.

Mixing colour

If we mix illuminatory colours, the result will be different from mixing pigment colours. When Issac Newton conducted his experiments for splitting light, he used all of the spectral colours to produce white light. Later experiments have shown that only three of the 'additive' primary colours need to be used to produce white light. These are orange–red, green and blue–violet. If three spotlights of these colours are shone together so that they overlap, where the three coincide, white light will appear; where two of the additive primaries combine, the secondary colours of cyan, yellow and magenta appear.

When working with pigment colour, a new set of rules applies. The primary pigment colours, which cannot be created from mixing other colours, are red, yellow and blue. If all three colours are mixed equally, grey would be created. The secondary pigment colours are orange, green and violet. These are produced by an equal mixture of two primaries. Orange is produced through mixing red and yellow; green is made when yellow and blue are mixed, and violet is a combination of blue and red.

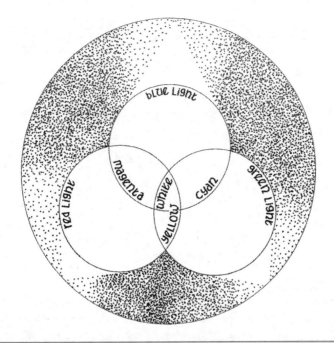

practice

1. secondary colours

You can experience mixing colours for yourself by making a coloured disc.

You will need a cork from a wine bottle, a matchstick, a 5-cm (2-inch) radius circle cut from cardboard, several circles of the same radius cut out of white paper and a small piece of double-sided tape. From the cork, cut a piece approximately 1 cm (½ inch) in length. Remove the flint from the end of the matchstick and taper the end of the matchstick to a point. Make a small hole in the centre of the cardboard disc and poke the matchstick through until 2 cm (¾ inch) is protruding on one side of the disc. Push the cork on to this by boring a small hole through its centre. On the opposite side of the cardboard disc, affix the small square of double-sided tape by

making a hole in its centre for the matchstick to pass through (see the diagram). You have now made a very simple spinning top.

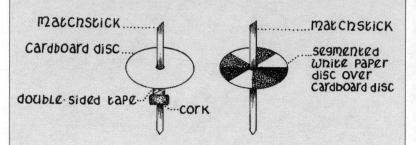

Divide each of the white paper discs into six wedge-shaped sections. Paint or colour the alternate sections on each of the paper discs with two of the primary colours. On one paper disc you may choose to use yellow and blue, on another red and blue. When you have completed this, make a hole in the centre of the disc to enable you to pass the longest end of the matchstick through. Finally, place the paper disc on to your spinning top and spin it on a flat surface. You should see the secondary colour appear.

This happens because the speed at which the top turns prevents the eyes from determining each colour separately. The brain therefore joins the two colours and produces the secondary colour.

2. TERTIARY COLOURS

If equal parts of the primary and secondary colour are mixed, the result is a tertiary colour. The primaries, secondaries and tertiaries make up the standard colour wheel. On this wheel, the arrangement of the colours follow the same order as the spectrum.

Colour the basic colour wheel with the colours given in each segment.

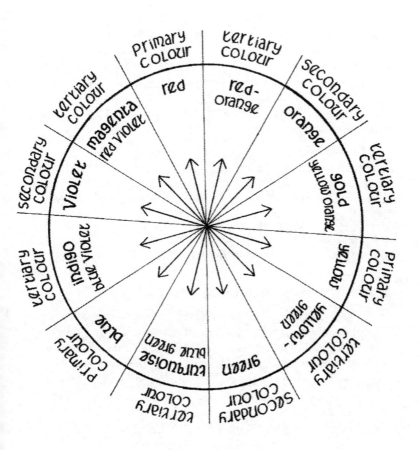

Each of the colours on the colour wheel has a complementary colour which can be found directly opposite it. Complementary pairs are those which, when mixed together in the same proportion, produce grey. This applies only to pigment colours.

To experience the complementary colour, take a piece of A5 paper and colour it with one of the colours from the colour wheel. When you have completed this, place it at a comfortable distance from your eyes. Stare at the paper until a corona of light appears around the outer edge. Now transfer your gaze on to a white wall or a second sheet of white paper. What you should see is the complementary colour appear. When you have achieved this, try transferring your gaze on to a piece of black paper, noting the difference.

This happens because the sensitivity receptors in the eyes, responsible for the colour that you have been gazing at, are reduced. This makes the other receptors more dominant, hence the reason for the appearance of the complementary colour.

The quality of the complementary colour, which you perceive when working with the above exercise, is similar to the auric colours which surround and interpenetrate all living things.

3. COLOUR HARMONY WHEEL

From white cardboard cut two circles. The first circle should be approximately 24 cm (9½ inches) in diameter. The second circle is slightly smaller. Inside each of these circles, draw a 7½-cm (3-inch) diameter circle. Divide the larger circle into twelve segments, starting from the outer rim of its inner circle. Paint or colour each of these segments with crayons of the appropriate colour, following the same order as given in the basic colour wheel. When you have completed this, take the slightly smaller circle and cut out two windows opposite each other. These should have the same dimensions as the segments on the larger circle and should extend from the rim of the inner circle to just inside the rim of the outer circle. Now lay the smaller circle on top of the larger circle and join them in the centre with a paper

pin. By rotating the upper circle, the colour with its
complementary colour will appear.

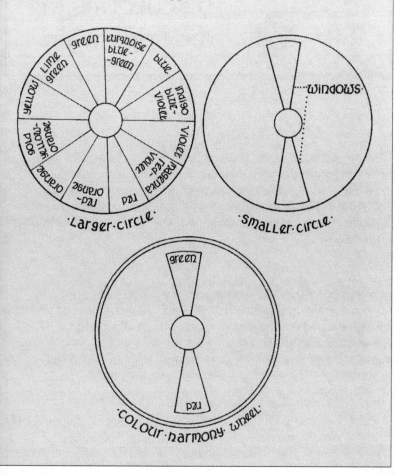

·Larger·circle·

·smaller·circle·

·colour·harmony·wheel·

3

THE COLOURS OF
THE SPECTRUM

*The world in which we live constantly surrounds us with colour.
It is displayed through nature, in fabrics and in interior design.
We, as human beings, have become so accustomed to its presence
that we fail to notice its beauty and have lost the ability to feel its
effect upon us. If only we could find time to 'tune in' to its healing
presence.*

Colour has the power to affect us physically, mentally,
emotionally and spiritually. How many times have you walked
through a wood of bluebells or into a garden filled with exotic
flowers and felt your spirits being lifted? How often is colour used to
express the way we feel: 'He was red with anger'; 'Green with envy';
'Yesterday she felt blue but today she is in the pink'?

No one has been able to provide a scientific explanation as to why
colour affects us emotionally. One theory is that when colour enters
the eye, it indirectly affects the emotional centre situated in the
hypothalamus. This in turn influences the secretions from the
pituitary gland, which then act on the other endocrine glands in the
body whose hormones dictate our moods and feelings.

Liking or disliking certain colours can be due to many things.
Intense like or dislike can sometimes be traced to happy or unhappy
childhood associations. Conversely, if you are aware and sensitive to
the power of colour, your attraction to certain colours may signify a
need for them.

If we do not work with colour, we rarely have the opportunity to develop an awareness in this field. But, if we want colour in our lives, we have to start looking afresh and begin to learn the colours which will give us the most benefit. In order to do this, let's look at the properties pertaining to each of the colours in the colour spectrum.

Red

On the electromagnetic spectrum, red falls next to infrared and, of the warm colours, red is the hottest. It has the longest wavelengths and lowest energy of all visible light. Red is a colour which demands attention. It is bold, imperative, provocative and creates excitement.

The names given to some of its shades are derived from the colour's source. Crimson and carmine originate from the Latin *kermesinus*, the name of the dye extracted from the kermes insect. Vermillion corresponds with the ancient name for mercuric sulphide, cinnabar. Ruby red stems from the root of the *rubia tinctoria* plant.

Red is equated with the heart, flesh and emotions. The emotions stimulated with this colour are love, courage, lust and rage. It is also linked with masculine energy and with aggression.

The planet Mars, known as the red planet, is named for the god of war. In China, the red flag symbolises revolution. The expression 'red with anger' rose from the belief that when a person becomes angry, the aura or electromagnetic field which surrounds him or her turns a dark shade of red.

Red is connected to life, most probably because it is the colour of blood. It was thought that blood held the secret of life, therefore the colour was credited with special powers. It is the colour associated with sexuality and with the arousal of sexual energy. Perhaps this is one reason why it is recommended for infertility.

Lust is one of its negative aspects. Phrases such as 'scarlet women' and 'red light district' expound this.

In order to see red, the lens of the eye has to adjust. The natural focal point of the eye lies behind the retina, so this makes red

objects appear to be closer than they really are. Likewise, a room painted entirely red would give the appearance of being smaller.

Physically, red increases the heartbeat, causes a release of adrenaline into the bloodstream and engenders a sense of warmth. For this reason it is helpful to wear red socks and gloves on cold hands and feet. According to Ronald Hunt in his book *The Seven Keys to Colour Healing* (see Further Reading), red splits the ferric salt crystals into iron and salt. The red corpuscles absorb the iron and the salt is eliminated by the kidneys and skin. This makes it a good colour to treat anaemia or iron deficiency. Although the red ray is low in energy, its effect on haemoglobin increases physical energy and improves the circulation.

This colour's power to constrict makes it unsuitable for asthmatics. Others that would not benefit from its qualities are those suffering from high blood pressure and those under stress.

Children tend to be attracted to red. The reason for this could be its earthing tendency. It is thought that a child does not fully integrate into the Earth's atmosphere until puberty. Although a child may love red, it is not a good idea to leave them for too long in an environment embracing this colour. It could cause them to become fractious.

When white is mixed with red, the result is pink. Although pink belongs to the red spectrum, it has the complementary attributes. It is a very gentle, feminine colour and is aligned to unconditional, spiritual love. Physically, it works well with the nervous system.

ORANGE TO BROWN

Orange is one of the colours associated with autumn. It is during this season that the leaves on trees turn to a blazing burnt orange before fading into the many shades of brown. It is thought that this colour gained its name from the orange fruit. The word 'orange' comes from the Arabic word *nananj* meaning fruit.

This colour is less dynamic and less aggressive than red. Whereas

red represents masculine energy, orange is the symbol of the gentler feminine energy, the creative energy.

Orange can have sexual connotations. This may stem from the fact that it is the dominant colour of the sacral energy centre, a centre associated with the female reproductive organs. In past eras, the orange seeds of the pomegranate were considered aphrodisiac and the custom of adorning brides with orange blossom was symbolic of fruitfulness.

Orange is a very joyful colour and has the power to give freedom to thoughts and feelings. Likewise it disperses heaviness in the physical body, allowing for natural, joyful movements. Also on a physical level, this colour, through its ability to bring about change in the biochemical structure, affords relief from depression. Furthermore, it has an antispasmodic effect which makes it a favourable colour for combating muscle spasms and cramp.

When orange darkens into brown, psychologically it becomes linked to comfort and security. Brown has been described as melancholy, gloomy and dull, but it can have its glamorous facets when portrayed in metal such as copper.

Brown is a very natural colour in its envelopment of earth and wood. It occurs throughout the animal kingdom, being a common colour for mammals. When worn by human beings, it can signify renunciation of the physical self, but can also be an outward display for a good organiser and disciplinarian.

Yellow to Gold

Yellow has the highest reflectivity of all colours and appears to radiate outwards, in contrast to blue and green which seem to recede. It is a colour connected to spring with the appearance of yellow daffodils, crocuses, primroses, forsythia and winter jasmine. Most yellow found in nature is caused chiefly by the pigment carotenoids and sometimes melanin. In fruit, yellow normally announces the presence of iron and vitamins A and C.

Yellow is the colour which represents light and is often used as the symbol for enlightenment. This is one of the reasons why Buddhist monks wear yellow robes.

The malign aspect of yellow is its connotation with cowardice. This could have arisen from sixteenth-century Spain where those people found guilty of heresy and treason were made to wear yellow before their ultimate fate of being burnt alive.

Pure yellow is a very happy colour. It radiates warmth, inspiration and a sunny disposition. It is associated with the intellect and with mental inspiration. Although this colour is beneficial in studies, to be surrounded by it for long periods could cause a state of mental and emotional detachment.

In England, bright yellow is not used extensively in fashion because of its clash with pink-toned skin. A bright yellow dress looks at its best in bright sunshine and on tanned or dark skin.

Yellow is a common colour in the animal world. When it is displayed in tropical fish, stinging insects and poisonous frogs, it acts as a warning colour.

The yellow rays carry positive, magnetic currents which are both stimulating and inspiring. This makes it beneficial to use with skin problems and for rheumatic and arthritic conditions.

A small amount of orange mixed with a bright yellow will produce a rich golden colour. The English word yellow is derived from the Indo-European *ghdwo* which is related to the word gold.

Gold is the most precious of metals. The Incas, people of a very ancient Peruvian civilisation, were sun worshippers and called gold 'the blood of the sun'. They were thought of as master goldsmiths. Craftsmen around the world use this metal to symbolise the glory of the heavens. In the Middle Ages it was highly prized for its quality of brightness and was used extensively in religious art, maybe because it was regarded as the colour of divinity. It was also used for its warmth, lustre and light-reflecting qualities to give mosaics vitality.

Gold, as an illuminatory colour, gives vitality and energy to the

human nervous system. It is therefore a great help to visualise this colour entering the body through the crown of the head and travelling through the body via the spinal vertebrae.

Green

Green is a colour of duality. It is composed from yellow, the last of the warm colours, and blue, the first of the cold colours. Green is associated with both life and decay. As life, it appears with the new foliage of spring; as decay, it is the colour displayed by the mould on rotting vegetation.

Egyptian mythology attributes this colour to Osiris, the God of vegetation and death. The Greeks linked it to Hermaphrodite, who is reputed to be the offspring of blue Hermes and yellow Aphrodite.

Green is the colour of balance and as such is able to engender stability to both mind and emotions. As human beings, we comprise body, mind and spirit and green has the power to bring these three aspects into balance to create a wholeness. It also works at integrating the left and right hemispheres of the brain. This colour is wonderful as a detoxifying agent and is beneficial for some heart problems.

During the day, when the cones of the eyes are working together, they are most sensitive to green light. The lens of the eye focuses green light exactly on the retina. This may be the reason why this colour is found to be very restful to the eyes. If you work for most of the day under artificial light, try to spend your lunch break amidst the varied greens of nature.

In the operating theatres of hospitals, green often abounds in the gowns worn by nurses and doctors and in the sheets which cover the patient. The complementary colour to green is red, and one theory put forward for its use in this way is to neutralise the after image produced by prolonged concentration on an open wound.

The negative qualities associated with green are nausea, poison, envy and jealousy. A person suffering seasickness is said to 'look green' and one overcome with jealousy is said to be 'green with

envy'. But for all this, the balancing properties pertaining to this colour are well worth working with.

PRACTICE

The best way of integrating green and balance into your life is through nature. Go out into the countryside and walk through green fields; sit beneath the green foliage of trees and breathe in the life-enhancing properties which are attributed to this colour. If it is warm, dry weather, walk barefoot to absorb the vibrational energy of this colour through your feet. The colour which nature gives us in abundance is green and there is surely a purpose for this.

Turquoise

Turquoise is made by mixing blue and green. Depending upon the proportions used, turquoise can veer towards either the blue or the green.

Turquoise was the national colour of Persia. The reason could be that it houses some of the oldest and finest turquoise gemstones. The Persian word for these gemstones is Piruseh, meaning joy. The ancient Persians believed that turquoise had a strong protective power and used the gemstones as charms to ward off evil.

Turquoise is the first colour to appear at the cold end of the spectrum. On a physical level, it is beneficial for reducing inflammation, in helping to strengthen the immune system and, like blue, in aiding insomnia.

Someone I know who works as a healer informed me that some of her clients who she has treated with this colour have experienced the presence of dolphins. I believe that these magnificent creatures are highly evolved and have tremendous healing power. I can well believe that in some extraordinary way they are associated with this gentle, soothing, healing colour.

Blue

The colour blue has an ancient, historic and symbolic association with royalty. A person descended from royalty is said to have 'blue blood'. This saying has a Spanish origin. They thought that the veins of aristocrats looked bluer than those with mixed ancestry.

In both the Greek and Roman Pantheons blue represented their respected gods, Zeus and Jupiter. In the Christian religion, the Virgin Mary is always depicted wearing a mantle of blue, signifying her status as 'Queen of Heaven'.

The expression 'blue-collar workers' originates from the dark blue clothing worn by Chinese peasants and industrial workers in the West. This colour was worn first because the dye was easily accessible, and second because it was thought that dark blue did not show dirt as easily as many of the other colours.

Although blue is a colour which suits most people and therefore is widely chosen in dress, in this respect it does have its negative aspects. The expression 'blue gown' was the name given to a prostitute, most probably because this was the colour dress that they were made to wear when entering a 'house of correction'. Maybe the title 'blue film' and 'blue language' stemmed from the same source.

Blue is a colour of inspiration, devotion, peace and tranquillity. These attributes make it a favourable colour to display in rooms set aside for therapy, relaxation or meditation. It is also a colour credited with lowering blood pressure.

Unlike red, this colour creates a feeling of space. It opens, as opposed to the constriction of red. This makes it a good colour for asthmatics. Because it possesses the qualities of peace and tranquillity, blue is an excellent colour for those suffering stress, tension, insomnia and high blood pressure.

On a physical level, the colour blue has few negative qualities and these are confined mainly to sadness and depression. Because of its ability to give the appearance of expansion, it can create a feeling of

isolation and solitude. To counteract this, its complementary colour orange can be used. The energy that these two colours promote is one of peaceful joy or joyful peace.

Indigo

A better-known name for indigo is 'denim' blue. This colour was originally derived from the hardy indigo plant which can be found growing in many parts of the world. This colour almost became extinct as a dye in the late 1940s, due to its dwindling popularity as a colour, and the expense of procuring the dye. It was the 'jeans' revolution in the 1950s that restored its popularity.

Indigo light is purported to be a potent painkiller; to have a powerful effect on mental complaints and the ability to psychologically clear and clean the psychic currents of the body.

As part of the blue spectrum, indigo therefore carries some of the blue rays' negative attributes. The main ones are its ability to promote depression, solitude and isolation.

This colour is the dominant colour of the brow chakra (see page 54) and because of this chakra's link with our intuition, indigo is reputed to enhance the ability to remember dreams.

Violet

Violet is the seventh colour belonging to the visible part of the electromagnetic spectrum. It has the shortest wavelengths and contains the highest energy. In the electromagnetic spectrum, it lies next to ultraviolet, a radiation which cannot be detected by human eyes.

In nature, there are flowers which radiate ultraviolet light. These attract those insects which see this light and are important in aiding the plant's pollination. Violet in nature is displayed by crocuses,

lavender, lilac and violets. In medieval times, the violet flower was looked upon medicinally. The oil extracted from these flowers was used as a sleeping draught. Today, oil of violets is still used to flavour drinks and confectionery as well as being utilised as a perfume.

Violet is a mixture of red and blue. In the medieval era, manganese oxide was the pigment used to make violet stained glass. As a dye, it was very expensive to produce which meant that it could be bought only by the wealthy. Perhaps this is the reason why violet was associated with royalty.

The psychological effects induced by this colour are self-respect, dignity and depth of feeling. It is a colour linked with spirituality, mysticism and insight. Violet can lead us into realms of spiritual awareness, where it becomes the gateway through which we must pass in order to become united with our true self or inner divine being.

Violet, composed of the vibrant energy of red and the calm, peaceful energies of blue, creates a balance out of these two colours. Because red is aligned to masculine energy and blue to feminine energy, violet has the power to balance these two energies found within each individual being. Only when this has been achieved are we able to have access to that wonderful cosmic sea of unconditional love.

The negative properties of this colour are connected with power used for manipulation and gain, and with abused sexuality.

Dr. Max Luscher in his book *The Luscher Colour Test,* (see Further Reading), states that emotionally immature and insecure people tend to be attracted towards this colour. He continues by saying that homosexuals and lesbians show a preference for this colour, highlighting their own emotional insecurity.

Magenta

Magenta is a combination of red and violet. The magenta dye was

first produced by the French who called it *fuchsine* after the fuchsia plant. It was renamed magenta by the Italians, after one of their villages near which an especially bloody Franco–Prussian battle was fought.

In fashion, this colour overtook violet in popularity during the later half of the nineteenth century. In the 1960s magenta was used in conjunction with orange to make what was referred to as a 'psychedelic' vibration. This symbolised ringing the changes and defying existing rules and regulations. The outward sign of this rebellion was the combination of these two opposing colours.

In the 1930s, a bright, strong, intense magenta was called 'shocking pink', in the 1950s it was 'hot pink', and in the 1960s 'kinky pink'.

On a physical, emotional and mental level, magenta is the colour of 'letting go', in order that change may take place. It assists us in letting go of old thought patterns born from conditioning, releasing old emotions which live in the past and giving up physical pursuits which we have outgrown. When we are able to do this, we free ourselves to flow with the tide of life. Only then can change, necessary for our spiritual growth, take place.

White

White is a colour containing all colours and which reflects all light. No natural substance is snow white. To obtain this degree of whiteness, the material has to be bleached. The oldest method of bleaching cloth was to spread it out on grass, under the sun. The oxygen given off by the green grass whitens, as well as strong sunlight and air.

White is associated with purity, innocence and change. The symbolism behind a white wedding gown was not purity and innocence alone, but also change. The change that the bride underwent in leaving her parents to start a new life with her husband.

White is representative of cleanliness and sterility. Until the 1960s

appliances used in the kitchen were invariably white. When used in doctors' and dentists' surgeries it proclaims a clean and sterile environment. This colour is purported to create distance and space which, when worn by therapists and medical practitioners, allows space between themselves and their patients.

White is abundant in nature. It is a colour portrayed by an endless variety of flowers. Animals who live in Arctic conditions are endowed with a coat of white fur. This acts as a camouflage when seen against the white snow.

This colour is strongly identified with spirituality. When able to transcend the physical mind, it has been related that the white light of consciousness dawns. Highly evolved souls are referred to as having 'reached a state of illumination'.

Very little negativity is associated with white. The small amount that is, for example 'a white lie' or 'white magic', is of a harmless nature.

Black

Black is the maximum darkness, the negation of all colour, but its totality is rare. In symbolism, black with its complementary white are literally the alpha and the omega, the good and the bad, day and night, birth and death.

In nature, this colour is exceptional. There are no natural black flowers. What appears to be black has been produced through human interference. To find an all-black animal is also unusual, but where black does occur in animals, it is generally given by the pigment melanin. It is the same pigment that colours the skin and hair of black races.

The negative connotations associated with this colour normally veer towards negativity and evil. We find this in sayings such as: the black arts, blackmail, the black sheep of the family, black mass, black looks ... the list is endless.

This colour's positive attributes are very seldom expressed. Black is

a colour which contains all things and out of which all things came. The darkness of the earth is the sacred womb which nurtures the germinating seed. Likewise the sacred darkness contained within the female uterus gives protection and nourishment to the growing foetus. Perhaps its ability to absorb all things is one of the reasons why young people, still trying to find their path in life, are attracted towards it.

GREY

A neutral grey is obtained when all spectral wavelengths are absorbed to the same degree. It is a colour which spans between black and white, and can enhance any of the other spectral colours.

Pure grey is very rare in nature. If you observe what appear to be grey rocks or animals, you invariably find at least one other colour present. In plants it appears in foliage as a silver grey.

We experience grey in clouds and in metallic objects. It is a colour which pervades the world of industry, being the dominant colour of machinery and the colour of most high-rise office blocks.

On a physical level it suggests intelligence, the grey matter of the brain, but it can also implicate confusion. If something is not black or white, then it must be a shade of grey. As well as confusion, it is indicative of fear. It has been reported that fearful people display patterns of grey in their aura.

OUR OWN AURA
OF COLOUR

Every human being is a microcosm within a macrocosm. The colours that we see displayed in nature are also displayed within the electromagnetic field or aura that surrounds each person. Looking at a person's aura is similar to looking through a kaleidoscope. The colours seen constantly change, creating ever new and awe-inspiring patterns. These colours and patterns are dictated by our health, thoughts and moods.

We, as humans, are beings of light and are unable to live without light. The light by which we live is derived from the sun in the form of *prana* or life force. This is in abundance on a bright sunny day and can be seen as minute globules of brilliant white light floating in the atmosphere. On a dull, grey day the amount available is reduced and at night it is almost non-existent. To compensate for the lack of night-time prana, the body stores it during the day. This is similar to the winter, when birds have to eat enough food during the day to provide the body fat needed to keep them warm and alive during the night.

According to Indian philosopher and yogi Swami Sivananda, 'prana is the sum total of all the energy in the universe'. It is the differentiated energy revealed in every possible form. Everything in the universe that moves is a manifestation of prana. Yogis affirm that what characterises life is its ability to attract prana to itself, to store it up and transform it for influence upon both the inner and outer world. They also affirm that it is in the air, yet it is neither oxygen nor nitrogen, nor any other constituent of the atmosphere. Prana exists in our food, water, sunlight, but is neither vitamin, nor

warmth, nor ultraviolet rays. Prana penetrates the whole body, even where air cannot reach. Prana is our true nourishment, for without prana there can be no life. The ancient Rishis proclaimed that prana can be stored in the nervous system, more particularly in the solar plexus which contains ganglia of nerve fibres.

In Western terms, prana on the physical plane can be described as vitality, as the integrating energy that co-ordinates the physical molecules and cells and binds them together. Were it not for the presence of prana, there could be no physical body as an integral whole, working as one entity. Instead, it would be nothing more than a collection of independent cells. According to Arthur E. Powell, author of *The Etheric Double*, (see Further Reading), prana, on the physical plane, builds up all minerals and is the controlling agent in the chemicophysiological changes in protoplasm, which leads to differentiation and the building of the various tissues of the bodies of plants, animals and men.

Knowing that we absorb prana from the food that we eat should make us aware of what we are eating. Junk food and food that is old, stale and containing a lot of preservatives is almost devoid of prana. As soon as fruit is picked and vegetables harvested, they start to decay and with this process, their life force diminishes. This is why it is important to eat as much fresh, organically produced food as possible. Likewise, if we drive a car and/or work in a big city, we are constantly breathing in pollution. To compensate for this, it is advantageous to go into the countryside whenever possible to breathe in the cleaner and more richly filled pranic air. This will vitalise and strengthen our physical body and auric field.

The human aura

The aura or force field surrounding a human person is ovoid in shape. The widest part is around the head and the narrowest around the feet. It resembles an egg sitting on its narrowest point. The aura is constantly expanding and contracting in a movement similar to the lungs when they inhale and exhale breath. Wearing synthetic

fibres restricts this movement, rather like wearing shoes that are too tight restricts the movement of the feet.

The aura constitutes seven layers, each of which interpenetrates with each other. These layers compose the physical body, the etheric sheath, the astral or emotional sheath, the mental sheath, the higher mental, the causal and the bodyless body. Although these layers interpenetrate each other, they remain individualistic. Each one works with a different aspect of our being and displays autonomous colours. These colours are normally dense near the physical body, gradually becoming more ethereal as they move towards the outer layers of the aura.

The outer layer – the bodyless body

This represents our true self, the part of us which has no beginning and no ending. It is the essence which knows all things, the divine part of us which has chosen to incarnate into a physical body to experience certain conditions only in existence on the Earth plane. Unfortunately, from the moment of birth, we are conditioned and this conditioning makes us forget the purpose for our present incarnation. To remedy this, we must learn to 'tune in' to our divine self. This is achieved through relaxation and meditation techniques.

The sixth layer – the causal

A record of all previous lives and the cause for our present incarnation are contained in this layer. Everything that we have done and are doing brings in the law of cause and effect. Christ said that whatever we sow so shall we reap. Yogic philosophy names this as karma and states that whatever good we do will be repaid by good; whatever evil, retribution will follow. This is the cause of some people during their lifetime experiencing a great deal of suffering for no apparent reason. Before incarnating, they chose how much of their karmic debt to repay.

The fifth layer – the higher mental

Here is the place where we are able to contact and listen to our

intuition. Although there are times when the information obtained from this source seems implausible, it is always correct. The hardest task is to learn to listen to and trust this begetter of wisdom.

The fourth layer – the mental

This is connected with the mind. Every thought that we think materialises as a thought form which is stored in this part of the aura. These forms can be projected into the atmosphere, to places and to people through visualisation. This is one of the methods used to transfer colour or divine light for absent healing. Like attracts like, therefore if we harbour negative thoughts, these will attract other negative thoughts of a like nature, thereby amplifying the negativity. If one is a very positive person, these thoughts will be augmented in the same way. This knowledge should teach us to be conscious of what we are thinking and to change any negativity to positivity. At first, this could prove difficult, but with practice and time, it can be achieved.

The third layer – the astral

Our emotional body is contained here, and registers, through the colours displayed, our feelings. For a majority of people, due to their inability to become the master and not the slave of their emotions, this part of the aura is frequently out of balance. I am sure that the sayings: 'red with anger'; 'green with envy'; and 'grey with fear' originated from the time when a high percentage of the population were able to see the aura. When a person is angry, dark red manifests in the aura, when envious it shows dark green and when afraid, patches of grey appear. With all the changes that are occurring with the advent of a new era, we are being challenged to gain mastery over this part of our being, but we have been given free will which leaves the choice to us.

The etheric layer

This layer of the aura contains the blueprint for the physical body and disintegrates alongside the physical body at death. Due to the interpenetration of the auric sheaths, our feelings, thoughts and

divine inspirations are registered here before manifesting at the physical level. Disease, which can be instigated from our mind and/or emotions, is seen in the etheric sheath as grey patches of accumulated energy. If this is not remedied, then it will be expressed as a physical disease.

The etheric part of the aura contains the very fine energy channels or *nadis* through which pranic energy flows. This network of infinitely intricate nadis establishes the counterpart of the entire nervous system.

The nadis

In the text *Gorakshasataka of the Nath Sect*, the guru Goraknath states that among the thousands of nadis that serve as carriers of prana, three are of prime importance. These are the pingala, ida, and sushumna. These three specific nadis are connected with conducting energy within the body.

Pingala is the positive line which channels the dynamic energy of prana. It is associated with the sympathetic nervous system which releases adrenaline to stimulate the superficial muscles. The sympathetic nervous system prepares the body to cope with stress and external activity.

Ida is the negative line, the channel of mental force. It is connected with the parasympathetic nervous system which sends impulses to the visceral organs to stimulate the internal process.

Sushumna, the third channel, functions partly as an earth wire, but the true purpose of Sushumna is to provide a channel for the great human spiritual energy force. It is said that when a person has integrated his or her physical, mental and spiritual aspects, this force rises to bring about enlightenment or God consciousness.

These three channels are symbolised as the caduceus, the symbol used by the medical profession. Many of the early pioneers of allopathic medicine, such as Hippocrates, acknowledged and worked with the subtle human anatomy. Unfortunately, with the

advent of drugs and advances in surgical procedures, this knowledge has been laid aside.

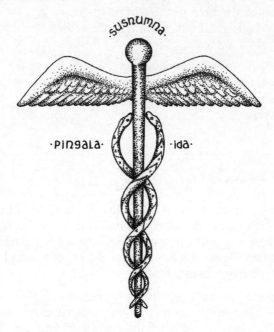

The chakras

As well as housing the nadis, the etheric sheath contains seven major and twenty-one minor energy centres, known in Sanskrit as *chakras*. It also contains numerous acupuncture points. A major chakra is defined by the crossing of twenty-one nadis; a minor chakra by fourteen nadis and an acupuncture point by seven nadis. These force centres can be found in each of the layers constituting the aura, but their prime importance is at the etheric level. They are both the transformers and the transmitters of energy for each of the layers.

In appearance they resemble a wheel. The word 'chakra' means a wheel or circle. The energies rhythmically pulsate and circulate

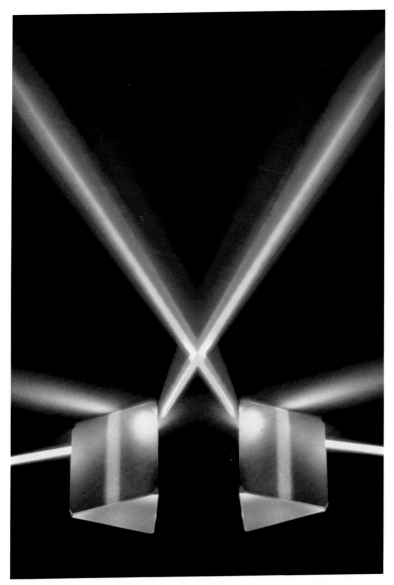

'From out of the darkness came the light
and the light and the darkness danced the dance of creation
and the colours of the spectrum were born.'

Gimbel

Additive colour (illumination)

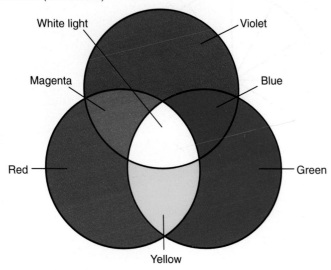

White light

Violet

Magenta

Blue

Red

Green

Yellow

Subtractive colour (pigment)

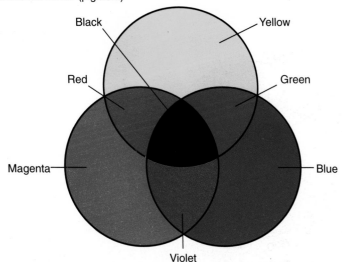

Black

Yellow

Red

Green

Magenta

Blue

Violet

When working with illuminatory light, mixing green, violet and red will result in white light. In subtractive or pigment colour, mixing yellow, blue and magenta produces black. The colours obtained when illuminatory colours are blended often differ from the same mixture of pigment colour.

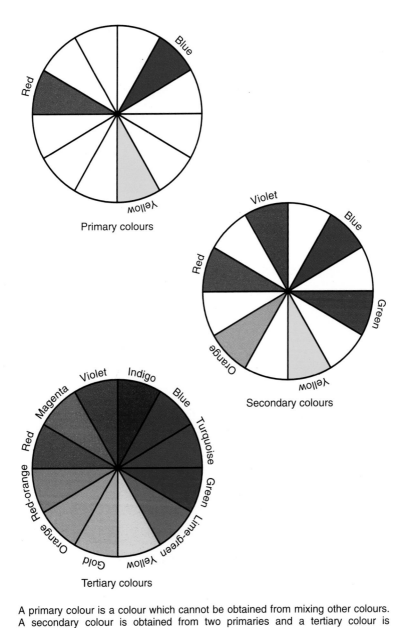

Primary colours

Secondary colours

Tertiary colours

A primary colour is a colour which cannot be obtained from mixing other colours. A secondary colour is obtained from two primaries and a tertiary colour is obtained by mixing a primary with a secondary colour.

In the beginning, God called forth the light and planted a tiny spark into the heart of all creation. As this light burns, it is diffused and rays out into the many colours of the spectrum. Each of these colours reveals one aspect of the personality, which must again become integrated into the light in order that a person may become whole.

through the hub of this wheel. These centres are never still, but the speed with which they rotate depends to some extent upon the state of health of the individual.

Five of the major chakras in the etheric sheath are in alignment with the spine, while the sixth and seventh are located between the eyebrows and just above the crown of the head, respectively. A chakra which is not acknowledged as one of the major centres, but is of prime importance, is the splenic chakra. It is this chakra which absorbs prana and disintegrates it into its seven varieties. Each of these seven varieties of prana vibrates to the frequency of one of the colours in the colour spectrum and establishes the dominant colour of the chakra to which it is distributed.

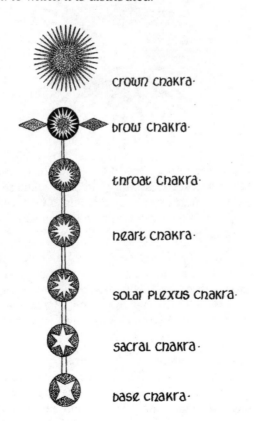

crown chakra·

brow chakra·

throat chakra·

heart chakra·

solar plexus chakra·

sacral chakra·

base chakra·

Each of the seven major chakras has a special link with one of the endocrine glands and with specific organs of the physical body. Each of these centres is also filled with symbolism. For more information on this refer to *Chakras for beginners*, by Naomi Ozaniec, in this series.

BASE CHAKRA

This chakra is situated at the base of the spine, its dominant colour is red and it has the slowest vibratory rate. It is related to the solidity of the Earth and therefore enables us to have our feet placed firmly on the ground. It is associated with the sense of smell and symbolised as a four-petalled lotus.

The parts of the body associated with the base chakra are the legs, feet, bones, large intestine, spine and nervous system. The endocrine glands with which it is related are the gonads; these are the ovaries in a female and testes in a male. I believe that this centre has a greater relationship with the male reproductive organs than with the female.

The mystical kundalini energy resides in this centre. This is symbolised as a curled snake. When a person reaches a specific place in his or her spiritual development, this energy is liberated to travel through the sushumna, piercing and awakening the

44

full potential of each chakra as she makes her journey to the crown chakra.

If the energies are not earthed in this centre, one can experience nervousness and insecurity. If the base chakra becomes blocked, and the reasons for this can be many, energy levels are low and problems could arise with the reproductive organs and with fertility.

Working with visualisation and Meditation

When working with visualisation and/or meditation, find a place which is comfortable and where you will not be disturbed. It is always beneficial to return to the same place each time you practise either of these arts. The still and peaceful energies which you generate will gradually build up, impregnating your chosen space and aiding you in your work. Try not to be discouraged if at first you find concentration difficult. The mind, for a vast number of people, is the master. What you are now trying to do is to reverse this so that you become the mind's master. If at first you experience difficulties, do not despair. Just relax and remember that practice makes perfect.

PRACTICE

When you are comfortably seated in your chosen place, make sure that your body is relaxed and comfortable. If it is not, move to a more comfortable position. Concentrate on your breathing, being aware of the slow and gentle inhalation and exhalation. If your mind starts to wander, gently bring it back to the task in hand. Be conscious of the thoughts passing through your mind. As you exhale, breathe these thoughts into the atmosphere, visualising them as beautiful bubbles which gently disintegrate.

Enveloped in this state of peace and relaxation, imagine that you are sitting or lying in a field. It is evening and the sun has just begun to sink below the horizon. The earth still radiates the warmth

taken from the heat of the day. As your gaze wanders across the sky, you become captured in the panoramic view of colour displayed. The golden oranges are turning to a bright luminous red which manifests its many hues as it fans away from the sun.

The redness of the sky becomes absorbed into the solidity of the earth, uniting them into a wholeness. You are aware that you have become part of this scenario. The red luminous cloak which surrounds you gives strength and warmth to your whole being. You feel this colour being absorbed into your base chakra and from there, radiating down your legs into your feet and out through your toes, back to Mother Earth. You feel the infinite wisdom of the Earth as she uses this colour that is now flowing through you to anchor you to herself, thereby giving you a firm and strong foundation upon which to grow and evolve as a spiritual being. Although we, as human beings, have treated her so badly by stealing her treasures and poisoning her with chemicals and pollution, she still tries to care for those who come into contact with her.

Shifting your gaze back to the sky, watch as the sun finally disappears and the deep indigo mantle of night shrouds the Earth.

Gently bringing your awareness back to your physical body, start to increase your inhalation and exhalation. Thank your higher self for all that you have been allowed to experience. Then, when you feel ready, gently open your eyes, stand up and stretch your body in readiness to continue the day.

SACRAL CHAKRA

The sacral chakra is found on the spine at the level of the sacrum. It is symbolised by a six-petalled lotus and radiates the colour orange. It is associated with the element Water and the sense of taste.

On a physical level, the sacral chakra influences the bladder, circulatory and lymphatic systems, the skin and female reproductive organs. The endocrine glands associated with it are the adrenals.

This centre is linked to creativity, especially in the female, due to its connection with the female reproductive system, through which a physical body is created for an incarnating soul. This centre has a close link with the creative energies at the throat chakra which displays this chakra's complementary colour, blue. When a woman reaches the menopause, the creative energies from the sacral chakra are transmuted to the throat chakra where they are transformed into creative spiritual energies.

When this centre is blocked, it can manifest as bladder and kidney disorders and circulatory problems. It can also result in a disfunction of either the male or female reproductive systems. In a male, this could show as premature ejaculation or the inability to achieve an erection. In a female it can result in the inability to reach orgasm, as infertility or in menstrual disorders.

When this chakra opens and starts to function to its full potential, it opens the powers of intuition and sensitivity. Some people initially find heightened sensitivity overpowering, but this will eventually find its balance on a higher evolutionary level.

PRACTICE

A lot of people, especially men, have lost touch with their creativeness. We live in a world governed by computer and scientific technology. All of this works with the intellectual left hemisphere of the brain. In order to bring about balance, we need also to work with the right, creative hemisphere. We can do this through art, dance, pottery, needlework, etc.

For this exercise, you will need a sheet of white paper and a set of coloured pencils or paints.

Go to your chosen place and, sitting quietly, relax your body and mind. Bring your concentration to the sacral chakra. Visualise this centre as a circle of pulsating, energising and creative orange light. If this proves difficult, try to imagine a shaft of clear orange light coming from the earth, through your feet, into your legs and into this chakra. Try to feel this chakra's size and then watch as the shafts of orange light radiate into your aura to strengthen and vivify it.

In your imagination, walk into the centre of this chakra. What does it feel like and what are you able to see? Are there other colours radiating from the heart of its centre or is the colour orange uniform throughout?

When you feel ready, gently bring your awareness back to where you are sitting. Breathe deeply before stretching your arms up over your head to bring your awareness back into your physical body. Using your sheet of paper and coloured pencils or paints, draw what you have experienced.

SOLAR PLEXUS CHAKRA

This centre is located on the spine at the level of the solar plexus and is depicted as a bright yellow lotus flower with ten petals. It is linked with the element Fire and the sense of sight. Fire gives the light which we need in order to 'see'. This applies not only to our

physical sight but also to our spiritual sight. The brightness of the Fire element at this centre governs the brightness of what we see.

At the level of the solar plexus centre we are able to experience warmth, expansiveness and joy. It is the centre of vitality in the psychic and physical bodies because it is here that prana (the upward-flowing vitality) and apana (the downward-moving vitality) meet, generating the heat that is necessary to support life.

At a physical level, this chakra is mainly concerned with the process of digestion. The organs which it influences are the breath, the diaphragm, the stomach, duodenum, gall bladder and liver. The endocrine glands with which it is associated are the islets of Langerhans, which form part of the pancreas.

The result of this chakra not functioning well is depression, rapid mood swings, poor digestion, abnormal eating habits, lethargy and nervous instability. There is an interaction between this centre, the sacral and the heart centre, therefore if it is blocked, sexuality cannot be connected to love. When the solar plexus chakra is open and functioning well, a deep and fulfilling emotional life is experienced.

PRACTICE

Go to your chosen place, sit down and start this session by relaxing your body and mind. Concentrate on your breathing. Start to breathe more deeply, making the inhalation the same length as the exhalation. If it helps, count to five or six as you breathe in and count to the same number as you breathe out. Do not hold the breath for any length of time. If you start to feel breathless or dizzy, resume normal breathing.

As you inhale, visualise a beam of golden yellow light coming through your feet into the solar plexus chakra. Exhaling, allow this light to circulate and penetrate every aspect of this centre. When your solar plexus has become filled with light, visualise this light as a golden sun, radiating warmth and energy to the parts of your body influenced by this chakra. Imagine one of the rays from your sun beaming down to connect with the sacral chakra and a second ray of light radiating up to connect with the heart chakra. This will allow all the creative aspects of the sacral chakra to function through unconditional love. Ask your higher self to allow you to see this with your inner sight and to understand through your inner tuition.

When you are ready, resume normal breathing. Bring your awareness back into your physical body. Sit and reflect for a few moments on your experiences before continuing with your day.

heart chakra

The heart chakra is located approximately at the level of the breastbone and slightly to the right of the physical heart. It is symbolised as a green lotus flower with twelve petals. It is affiliated to the element Air and to the sense of touch.

The Sanskrit word for this centre is *anahata*, which translated means 'the unstruck'. All sound is created by the vibrations from the

interaction of objects. The sound manifesting from this chakra is the primordial sound which originates beyond this world.

This is the centre where we experience love. Love has one of the highest vibratory rates, and how we experience this depends upon how open and evolved this centre is. Love can be felt at a purely physical level, either as sexual arousal or lust, but as we evolve spiritually, it is transformed into an unconditional love which encompasses all things. Before reaching this state, we have first to learn to love all aspects of ourselves. When this has been achieved, we slowly start to become the unconditional love which is able to reach out to all beings and conditions which we encounter, without judgement.

On a physical level, the heart chakra is associated with the heart and circulatory system, the lungs and respiratory system, and the arms and hands. The endocrine gland assigned to it is the thymus.

If this chakra malfunctions, it can lead to a disorder in any parts of the physical body that it is identified with.

PRACTICE

Go and sit quietly in your chosen place. Relax your body and still your mind.

When you feel relaxed and at peace, withdraw into yourself. Ask yourself how much you are able to love all aspects of your being. Can you love and accept your thoughts, whether they are of a positive or negative nature? Can you love your feelings, especially when they are not very harmonious? Can you love your physical body; its shape, size and any deformities that may be present? A lot of people have been taught that it is wrong and selfish to love themselves, but if we cannot love ourselves, can we truly love anyone else? We may be able to on an intellectual level, but it is not possible from our heart centre.

Bring your awareness into the heart centre. Visualise this as a circular space filled with pale green light. In the centre of this space lies the bud of a pale pink rose. As you stand before the rose bud, it opens and streams of the pale pink light of unconditional spiritual love flow from its petals. Consciously direct this pale pink light to any part or aspect of yourself that you find difficult to love. Imagine this colour dissolving any barriers which have been erected through conditioning, and that you feel are no longer right for you. Fill the space left by the barriers with this pale pink light.

Finally, allow this light to saturate the space where you are sitting so that when you next return, you will automatically be surrounded by these vibrations.

When you are ready, bring your awareness back to your physical body. Slowly start to increase your breathing. When you are ready, open your eyes.

THROAT CHAKRA

The throat centre is located on the spine at throat level. It is symbolised by a blue sixteen-petalled lotus flower and is related to the element Ether. Alchemists refer to Ether as the mixing bowl in which the elements of the four lower chakras are formed.

This centre is related to the spoken word; to sound. The sound produced here is normally governed by one of the four lower elements. If the voice is heavy and unresponsive, it comes from the Earth of the base chakra; if it is soft and sexual, it comes from the sacral chakra; a warm and passionate voice belongs to the Fire of the solar plexus chakra, and if it is gentle and sympathetic, it originates from the heart chakra.

The throat chakra forms the bridge over which we must cross to pass into the spiritual realm. It is also the bridge between the four lower elements and the principle of thought at the brow chakra.

Yogic philosophy teaches that the throat chakra is where divine nectar is tasted. This nectar is a sweet secretion produced by the lalana gland near the back of the throat. When this gland is stimulated by higher yogic practices, it is claimed that its nectar can sustain a yogi for any length of time without food or water.

On a physical level, this chakra governs the nervous system, the female reproductory system, the vocal cords and the ears. The endocrine glands with which it is affiliated are the thyroid and parathyroids.

PRACTICE

Go and sit quietly in your chosen place. Relax the body and still the mind. Take a few slow, deep breaths, exhaling any tension and persistent thoughts bombarding your mind.

Bring your awareness to the throat chakra and visualise the soft blue light radiating from it. Picture this colour flowing from this centre into your aura, creating around you a cloak of peace and protection.

Return your thoughts to the throat and allow yourself to verbally produce any sound which you feel is right for you. It does not matter if the sound you make is loud, soft, melodious or discordant. Just allow sound to flow from you. When you feel ready, shift your awareness to each of the lower chakras in turn, starting with the base chakra. With each of these lower centres, try to produce the sound which describes their present condition. If you practise regularly, you will be surprised how the sound changes from day to day.

Colour and sound have a very close affinity to each other. Therefore, each chakra vibrates to a sound as well as a colour. Working with either of these vibrations will help to balance the chakras. The sounds connected with these centres are governed by how spiritually awake a person is and will therefore be slightly different for each individual.

When you are ready, gently increase your breathing, open your eyes, stand up and have a good stretch before continuing your day.

BROW CHAKRA

The brow centre is located on the forehead, between the eyebrows. It radiates the colour indigo and is frequently depicted as a two-petalled lotus. These two petals speak of the duality of human nature; the yin and the yang and the masculine and feminine energies which are inherent in all human beings. At this centre,

when it is fully opened, the duality is integrated into wholeness. When this has been achieved, a person has control or command over the personality or lower self.

The brow chakra likewise reflects the twofold nature of the mind – the ego self and the spirit self; the reasoning and the intuitive mind.

On a physical level it is related to the eyes, nose, ears and brain. The endocrine gland with which it is associated is the pituitary.

If this chakra is out of balance, it can lead to sinus problems, catarrh, hay fever, sleeplessness, migraine, tiredness and irritability. A hindrance to the free flow of this centre is rigid thoughts, not allowing ourselves to look at other ideas and opinions and, if need be, change or modify our own.

PRACTICE

Go and sit in your chosen place. Relax the body and still the mind from unwanted thoughts.

Concentrate on the brow centre. Remember that this is the centre of both physical and spiritual mind. It is the centre which is brought into play when we work with visualisation or meditation.

As you concentrate on this centre, try to visualise the vastness of the Earth, sky and space. Look with great love upon all that you see with your inner sight. Try to recognise both the male and female

energies within you. Are you able to accept both of these equally? Think about the intellectual and creative hemispheres of the brain. Are you integrating both of these into your life? The yin and yang energies are kept balanced through diet. Are you eating a well-balanced, healthy diet? It is only when we become aware of these energies that we are able to look within ourselves and discover changes that need to take place. These changes work towards integrating this duality.

When you are ready, bring your awareness back to everyday consciousness. Think about changes which you need to make and then plan the best way for this to happen. You might find it useful to keep a personal diary of your experiences and to record which way forward you feel is best for you.

CROWN ChAKRA

The crown centre is located at the top of the head and contains the highest energy frequency. It is symbolised by a thousand-petalled lotus-radiating violet.

The vibration at this centre is often depicted by artists as a halo around highly evolved beings. When one is centred in this chakra,

the lower and higher self have been united, enabling us to experience the indescribable bliss of union with one's own source; the divine reality within our own consciousness. In order to obtain this state, we have to renounce the illusory self. When we are able to do this, we find our true self which corresponds to the transmutation of the energies from the lower chakras to the crown.

On a physical level, this chakra is related to the pineal gland. This is the gland which is activated during meditation and is sometimes referred to as the hallucinatory gland.

PRACTICE

Go and sit quietly in your chosen place. Gently relax the body and quieten the mind.

Bring your concentration to the top of your head. Visualise yourself standing outside a many-petalled violet flower. At the centre of the flower sits a many-faceted diamond. Each face of the diamond represents a part of you. Included are your thoughts, relationships, home life, work, etc. Also represented is your past and future.

Looking at the diamond, you observe that some of its facets glow less brightly than others. These are the facets which have been masked from the light of the spiritual sun. Look at them more closely and you will perceive that they represent the things that are no longer right for you and therefore need to be changed. These could be past memories or relationships which you are hanging on to; it could be fear of the future; insecurity or loneliness. Take this time to look into yourself and ask to receive the courage to let go of the things which are no longer relevant in your life. This can be likened to clearing the junk and cleaning the attic to let the light shine through. The more we are able to do this, the more we are able to make contact with our higher self, that tiny droplet from the vast ocean of cosmic light and love.

When you are ready, bring your awareness back to your physical body. Gently increase your breathing before opening your eyes.

5

USING COLOUR FOR SELF-HELP

Colour is a wonderful medium for helping us in the many aspects of our lives. It can be used for healing; for relaxation; for stress reduction; for spiritual growth and awareness; and to enhance any path that we are following. In whatever way and for whatever purpose we use it, to experience its positive attributes we must practise on a regular basis. If you really want colour to work for you, I would suggest that you set aside the same time each day to work with one of the given techniques.

Colour, used as a therapy, is still in its infancy of rediscovery. Because we are beings of light and are surrounded and interpenetrated by the colours of refracted light, these colours can be used to restore a state of harmony. If you are unwell and wish to be treated with the vibrational frequencies of colour, it is always advisable to seek the help of a qualified colour practitioner. It is equally recommended that you seek medical advice in order to know what you are dealing with. There are medical conditions whose symptoms seem trivial but which require prompt medical attention.

At the end of this chapter is a chart listing the colours which are beneficial for minor problems. These colours can be utilised with any of the techniques explained in this chapter. Should the problem not respond after two days, seek the advice of your doctor.

COLOUR BREATHING

When inhaling, we breathe in prana or life force. Prana encompasses

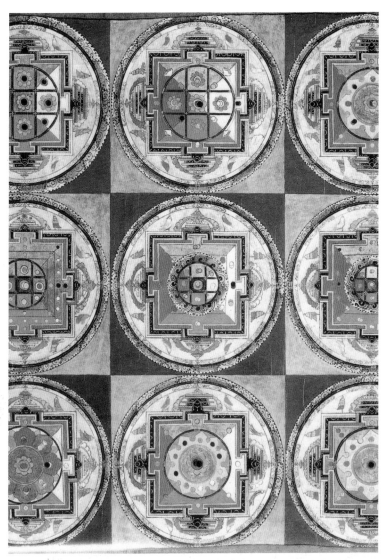

The mandala born, thus, of an interior impulse became, in its turn, a support for meditation, an external instrument to provoke and procure such visions in quiet concentration and meditation. The intuitions which, at first, shone capricious and unpredictable are projected outside the mystic who, by concentrating his mind upon them, rediscovers the way to reach his secret reality.

Theory and Practice of the Mandala by Giuseppe Tucci

The wonderful and uplifting illuminatory colours portrayed in stained glass bring healing to the soul and enable one to transcend to the white light of God consciousness. This is the South Rose Window in Reims Cathedral, France, dating from the thirteenth century.

'A human being is a part of the whole called by us "the universe", apart, limited in time and space. He experiences himself, his thoughts and feelings, as something separate from the rest – a kind of optical illusion of his consciousness. This delusion is a kind of prison for us, restricting us to our personal desires and affections for a few persons nearest to us. Our task must be to free ourselves from this prison by widening our circle of understanding and compassion to embrace all living creatures and the whole of nature in its beauty.'

Albert Einstein

Throughout the ages, humans have used colour in a variety of ways. This picture shows how tribes use colour to adorn their bodies. The meaning relates to the colours used depending upon which tribe they belong to. This man is of the Mumunga people of Papua New Guinea.

seven varieties, each of which vibrates to the frequency of one of the spectral colours. Therefore, when we work with colour breathing, we visualise inhaling the colour which we feel we need. We can either imagine the colour saturating our whole being or we can mentally direct the colour to the part of the body where we feel it is needed.

When working with this technique, visualise red, orange and yellow entering the body through the feet; green entering horizontally at heart level, and turquoise, blue, indigo, violet and magenta entering through the top of the head.

Try to breathe in for the same length of time as you breathe out. Try to make the breath slow and smooth. If at any time during the exercise you become breathless or giddy, immediately resume normal breathing.

PRACTICE

Go to your chosen place. Relax your body and quieten your mind.

Allow your concentration to rest at the base chakra. As you inhale, visualise a ray of pure red light coming through the soles of your feet into this chakra. Exhaling, allow this colour to radiate from the chakra, into your aura, down your legs and feet and back to the earth. Try to feel the warmth and energy that this colour brings.

Move your awareness into the sacral chakra. This time as you inhale, imagine a ray of clear orange light coming through the soles of your feet, up your legs into this chakra. As you breathe out, watch this colour spread into your aura, creating a wonderful sense of joy and happiness.

Now concentrate on the solar plexus chakra. On the next inhalation, picture a ray of clear yellow light coming through the soles of your feet, up your legs into this chakra. See the whole of this area turning into a golden sun of pulsating energy. Breathing out, watch the rays from this sun extend into your aura.

Next, move to the heart chakra. Breathing in, envisage a ray of

clear green light horizontally entering this chakra. As you exhale, and the green light spreads into your aura, allow it to balance any aspect of yourself that is disordered.

Shift your concentration to the throat chakra and breathe a ray of clear blue light, through the top of your head, into this chakra. As you breathe out, watch this colour swirl into your aura, bringing peace and tranquillity to the physical body. Imagine this colour to form a cloak of protection around you, keeping at bay any negative energies.

Take your awareness to the brow chakra. Breathe a clear ray of indigo light, through the top of your head, into this chakra. Ask this colour to give you a clearer insight into any path that you may be following and to clarify any doubts that you may have. Exhaling, allow this colour to expand into your aura.

Finally, concentrate on your crown chakra. As you inhale, visualise a ray of clear violet light entering this chakra. As you exhale this colour into your aura, let it give you the self-respect and dignity which is rightly yours, and let it help you to love all aspects of yourself.

When you are ready, bring your awareness back to your physical body; deepen your breathing before gently opening your eyes.

Visualisation

When working with the body/mind relationship, visualisation can play a vital role. Frequently visualisation and imagination are expressed as the same thing, but there is a very distinct, although slight, difference between them. Visualisation is the ability to call up a clear visual image, and imagination is the faculty for forming images in the mind.

When starting to work with visualisation, for most people it is their imagination that comes into play. This, with practice, patience, personal growth and sensitivity, is eventually transformed into visualisation.

The process of working with colour through visualisation helps transform negative aspects of ourselves into positive ones. This can enhance our well-being and help us along our chosen path in life. Like most things, if we are to experience the positive attributes of colour visualisation, practice has to be on a regular basis, and we have to believe in what we are doing. Doubt creates a barrier which halts the transforming process.

PRACTICE

Lying on your bed, make sure that you are comfortable and warm. Bless the day that has just passed as you turn over to a new page in your book of life, enabling you to start tomorrow afresh.

Be aware of the silence that night brings. Inhale this stillness and silence into your own body and mind so that they may relax. Surrender to the night the stress and weariness that the day has brought.

Visualise your bed turning into a fluffy white cloud that gently lifts and floats you out into the night air. The night owl and other nocturnal creatures are the only souls about, on the prowl for food and sport. Snug and warm on your fluffy white cloud, you are able to see the myriad stars stretching far out into the universe and hear the gentle modulating harmonies which create their symphony. Experience these sounds balancing and relaxing your own physical body as they resonate with your body's own sound. The deep indigo night sky forms a mantle of peace and protection around you, permitting you to gently drift into the re-energising realm of sleep that prepares you for the dawn of a new day.

MEDITATION

The world in which we live is full of strife, pain and disharmony. The pace of life gets faster with each passing year. Changes are rapidly occurring both in the world and within ourselves. Meditation is the art of transcending this turmoil in order to find our true self where peace, security and unconditional love dwell.

The seven chakras described in Chapter 4 can be likened to doors which lead to higher levels of consciousness. When working with meditation, these doors open to allow us through. It is therefore extremely important that we close them at the end of each meditation. One way of doing this is to visualise a circle of light surrounding an equally limbed cross of light. This symbol is then used as the key to close each chakra. At the end of a meditation, starting with the crown chakra, place this symbol around each of your chakras, picturing each one closing.

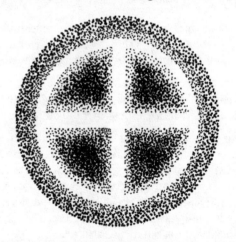

PRACTICE

Sit down in your chosen place and relax your body and mind.

Imagine that you are sitting in a glass bulb-shaped chalice. This chalice is wide at the bottom and narrow at the top, similar to a brandy glass. The way in which it has been made enables it to reflect all the colours of the spectrum. As the light passes through the glass, the space between you and the chalice is filled with red, orange, yellow, green, blue, indigo and violet, colours which are constantly playing and dancing with each other. The chalice is strong and forms a protective web around you and its colours of ethereal light represent your aura.

Looking up to the opening at the top of the chalice, visualise a shaft of white light flooding into your crown chakra and overflowing into the lower chakras. This resembles a tiered waterfall of light. As each chakra becomes filled to overflowing, you become filled with energy and light enabling you to become a pure, clear channel for healing, a channel of light and joy.

When you are completely filled with light, spend a few moments in silence, thanking the spiritual realm for this gift and listening for any message that spirit wishes to convey to you.

When you are ready, start to increase your breathing, close down your chakras as described at the beginning of this section and open your eyes.

Coloured clothing

Colour can be absorbed into our being through the clothes we wear. These act as a filter through which light passes. If you are working with colour in this way, then white must be worn underneath the coloured garment. Failing this, the article of clothing can be worn next to the skin with nothing covering it.

The more sensitive we are to the vibrational energies of colour, the more we are able to discern which colour we need at any one time. I am sure that you have experienced being drawn towards a colour one day but repelled by it the following day. When we are drawn towards a colour, it is indicative of our need for the energies of that colour. When we have satisfied our need, we no longer feel attracted to it. Most of us are dictated to by the colours that are in fashion in any given season, but unfortunately these fashionable colours are not necessarily the ones that we need for our well-being.

There is a branch of colour teaching which ascribes individuals to the colours related to the seasons of the year. They are termed as a spring, summer, autumn or winter person. The colours which are selected for individuals are the ones which enhance their skin tone.

This is a valid way of working with colour, but unfortunately its methods cannot be used when working therapeutically with colour.

Coloured scarves or swatches

Another way of working with colour is with full-length, coloured scarves and swatches. These are placed over the part of the body needing colour. When working with this technique, the material used should be either cotton or silk. Both of these are natural fibres and more inducive to the healing process.

Practice

Stress and/or insomnia

Obtain a piece of blue, full-length material in either cotton or silk. Lie beneath this, in a warm, light room, for twenty minutes each day. For this exercise you need to wear white or, if it is in the privacy of your own home, you can be naked.

Sore throat

For this you will need a turquoise silk scarf. Wrap this around your neck until your throat starts to heal. I know from experience that this works.

Eye strain

If you suffer tired or sore eyes, especially if this is caused through working with a UVD screen, place a piece of thin, indigo cotton over your eyes and relax for fifteen minutes.

ABSORPTION OF COLOUR THROUGH FOOD

The natural colour displayed in the food we eat is a further way of taking colour into ourselves. When preparing food, try to include as many colours as possible in the meal. Make sure that the colours presented are natural and not obtained from dyes. It is alarming how many of the foods found on the supermarket shelves have been doctored in one way or another. These additives are usually chemically based and toxic to our bodies.

FRUITS AND VEGETABLES DISPLAYING THE SPECTRAL COLOURS	
Colour	**Fruit and vegetables**
Red	Cabbage; tomatoes; radishes; beetroot; red peppers; red cherries; raspberries, redcurrants; red plums.
Orange	Carrots; swedes; pumpkins; orange peppers; mangoes; apricots; oranges; tangerines.
Yellow	Yellow peppers; parsnips; marrow; sweetcorn; cheese; yolk of an egg; golden plums; pineapple; grapefruit; honeydew melon; lemons.
Green	Green peppers; spinach; cabbage; lettuce; watercress; peas; runner beans; green lentils; greengages; kiwi fruit; green apples.
Blue	Grapes; bilberries; blue plums; grapes.
Violet	Aubergine; purple broccoli; purple grapes; plums.
Magenta	Strawberries; deep pink cherries.

Colour through nature

To me, one of the most beneficial ways to experience colour is through the living, vibrant colours of nature. Try to spend at least one hour a week walking through parks, the countryside or sitting in your own garden. If you have a garden, walk or sit barefoot on the grass. This will enable you to absorb the earth energies through your feet and the colours of nature through your eyes. I have walked barefoot across a frost-covered field. Initially, it felt very cold, but I was amazed at the amount of energy gleaned from this exercise.

When you start to work with colour, try all of the suggestions in this book and any that you discover yourself. This will enable you to find the method that works best for you.

COLOURS THAT CAN BE USED FOR MINOR AILMENTS		
Colour	**Complementary colour**	**Minor ailments**
Red	Turquoise	Cold hands or feet Low blood pressure To earth oneself
Orange	Blue	Lack of energy Depression
Yellow	Violet	Skin complaints Arthritis Indigestion To aid mental pursuits
Green	Magenta	To balance the yin and yang To detoxify any part of the body To balance all aspects of being

Turquoise	Red	To boost the immune system To reduce inflammation Sore throat
Blue	Orange	To reduce stress To release tension High blood pressure Insomnia
Indigo	Gold	Headaches Eye strain Neuralgia
Violet	Yellow	To help us to love and respect ourselves
Magenta	Green	To help with any change that is taking place in our lives In letting go of conditioning and situations which hinder our progress in life

COLOUR EXPRESSED THROUGH ART

In art, colour is used to create space and light. Optical science has shown that blue creates an impression of receding, while red tends to give the impression of advancing. If we look into nature, we will discover that colours lose their intensity and distinctness the further they recede into the distance. This is due to atmospheric conditions. The short wavelengths of blue travel through the atmosphere more easily than the long wavelengths of red. This is the reason for colour appearing paler and bluer towards the horizon.

ART THROUGH THE AGES

Since the beginning of time, we have expressed ourselves through the media of art. This has ranged from simple cave drawings to exquisitely coloured landscapes. The techniques and colours used were determined by their availability.

The materials available to prehistoric artists were very limited. The colours that they used were those that could be obtained from the earth: white from chalk and the calcite crystals which lined the inside of caves; red, brown and yellow from ochre; black from charred wood. To make these materials workable, they were mixed with animal fat and then warmed.

As the human race evolved, we learnt how to make dyes from animal products, plants and minerals. Those made from minerals were brilliant and lasting, but those derived from animal products and plants faded when exposed to light. From this came the knowledge to produce synthetic dyes and a wider range of colours.

Most of the early civilisations had adopted specific colours into their culture. Typical early Egyptian colours were white, black, turquoise, green, red, ultramarine blue, yellow ochre and brown. Green they produced from malachite and Egyptian blue was a compound of silica, copper and calcium. For a short time, they made brown by grinding up embalmed bodies. This acquired the colour the name of 'mummy brown'.

The early Romans' speciality was bright red. They made this colour from the cinnabar mined in Spain. The other colour with which they were associated was Tyrian purple, but the exorbitant cost of producing this colour turned it into a symbol of wealth. Another disadvantage was its tendency to turn black when exposed to light.

Some theorists tried to link early Italian paintings with the planets and with the elements of nature. They identified red with Fire, blue with Air, green with Water, and grey with Earth. In spite of this, the Italians' most prized colour was ultramarine blue. This was made from lapis lazuli and was extremely expensive to produce. The only colours thought to equal its intensity were vermillion and pure gold.

Gold, a very precious and expensive metal, has been used by artists worldwide. Owing to its natural impurities, it usually has a slightly green hue. To give it a warmer appearance, it was underlayed with red clay. Gold has been used worldwide to portray mysticism and things related to the heavenly sphere. An example is the gold halos surrounding the heads of saints and enlightened beings. To use gold leaf in a painting or fresco, the surface had to be prepared before the overlapping layers were applied. When complete, it was smoothed and polished with a burner.

In the early fifteenth century, the refinement of oil painting opened up an almost unlimited range of colour possibilities. A technique was used whereby powdered pigment was mixed with a slow-drying oil. The advantage gained from this was the ability to easily fuse and blend the colours.

Colours in art became revolutionised in the mid-nineteenth century by Impressionist artists such as Claude Monet. Their paintings depicted nature in her many moods and ever-changing colours. The colours which these artists used were bright and encompassed the complementary hues. As the century moved to its close, poetic art was revived, conveying emotional, sensual and spiritual experiences.

By the early twentieth century, abstract art had come into fashion. This form of art relies on the dynamic nature of colour and often bears no likeness to anything seen in the outside world. The colour is used in unconventional ways, frequently poured or splattered on to canvas and spread with unconventional tools.

Art as therapy

Whatever the style or technique adopted in art, it can be therapeutic. Through the creative media of colour, we are able to express on paper our thoughts, feelings and spiritual aspirations. These can be of a negative or positive nature. Through this act of expression, tension and stress are worked through, which could, if not released, result in some form of disease. We do not have to be great artists to work in this way. The only requirements are paper and a set of coloured pencils or crayons.

Art therapy was first practised in England during the 1940s, mainly as a result of the work of the artist Adrian Hill and psychotherapist Irene Champernowne. While recovering in hospital from tuberculosis, Adrian Hill passed the time drawing and painting. He encouraged other patients to do the same, hoping that it would distract their minds from their present conditions and from their traumatic wartime experiences. To his surprise, Hill discovered that they were expressing their fear and trauma through their art.

Irene Champernowne studied psychotherapy under the Swiss psychoanalyst Carl Gustav Jung. Through Jung's methods of using painting and modelling to help patients express their unconscious feelings, she found help through her own emotional crisis. After qualifying through the Jungian School, she and her husband started a centre for 'psychotherapy through the arts'.

Another pupil of Jung's, who became one of the leading practitioners of art therapy in Britain, was Rita Page Barton. In an article, published shortly after her death in 1986, she wrote: 'The therapeutic value of the arts in eliciting the patient's own healing powers is constantly shown and never fails to be awe inspiring'.

Since those early beginnings, art therapy has steadily grown, and today is practised in many parts of the world.

As the early pioneers experienced, this form of therapy helps people to communicate their thoughts and feelings visually. Some of the fears and anger expressed have been so deeply buried that the person is no longer aware of them. Giving these a visual form is often the first step in the healing process. It is only when we recognise a problem that we are able to work to overcome it.

Initially, a person who has not worked in this way may find difficulty in working spontaneously to express feelings. But, once a start has been made, the person normally becomes so engrossed in what he or she is doing, that any fears and inhibitions are forgotten, enabling more freedom of expression. If this is your first attempt, you might find yourself producing random splodges of colour or nervous doodles. Don't give up on the pretext that it does not work for you. All worthwhile pursuits take time and patience to master.

If you are unwell or under great stress, you might prefer to work under the auspices of a qualified art therapist. Sometimes, this form of therapy is worked at in a group situation. Each group consists of about eight to ten members. Each member works individually, but is encouraged to help other members and to work on group projects. Group art therapy is recommended for people who have difficulty in relating to others or who suffer ailments such as alcoholism, drug addiction, anorexia or bulimia.

Even if you are well and are not aware of feeling under stress, working with art in this way can be a very interesting exercise. If we are familiar with a therapeutic technique, it is easier to apply it when needed. Another advantage of this is that you have the materials to hand when and if required.

PRACTICE

For this exercise, you will need white paper, and a set of colour pencils or crayons.

Often, during the course of a day, things do not always go according to plan. This can leave us feeling irritable, hurt, angry or frustrated. These feelings are either kept inside ourselves or vented at those nearest to us. Next time this happens to you, find a quiet corner and work out your feelings by expressing them on paper with your coloured pencils. What materialises may be a series of jagged, black and red knotted lines. Don't let this worry you. You are the only person who is going to see the drawing, unless you choose to share it with another, and you can immediately destroy it if you wish. It is far better to release any negative feelings in this way, than to store them inside yourself where they could eventually manifest as a physical disorder.

Therapeutically expressing sound through colour

Colour and sound have a great affinity with each other. The vibrational frequency of each sound is akin to the frequency of one of the hues found in the colour spectrum. This turns each melody, symphony and opera into a creative, ever-changing landscape of colour as well as an all-embracing cacophony of sound.

PRACTICE

For this exercise, you will need some white paper, a set of coloured pencils or crayons and two music tapes. One of these tapes should contain your favourite classical music and the other a piece of jazz, pop or rock music.

Find a place which is quiet and where you will not be disturbed. Select and play one of the two tapes. As you listen to the music, choose the colours which you think fit the mood of the music, then express on the paper the feelings that the music evokes in you. After approximately fifteen minutes, change tapes and repeat the exercise.

When you have finished both drawings, compare them, trying to discover what emotions, thoughts and aspirations the music has elicited in you and take note of how you have formulated these in your drawings.

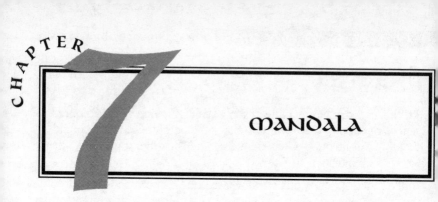

MANDALA

Another way of working creatively with colour is through mandalas. The literal translation of the Sanskrit word mandala is 'circumference, centre or magic circle'. To create a mandala, two things are needed. The first is a circle and the second a central point.

The circle is formed from a line that has no beginning and no ending, making it the symbol of eternity. The centre point represents unity, perfection and our own individual and divine self.

Mandalas were used as a healing art by Hindus, Tibetan Buddhists and native Americans before they were introduced into our Western society. It was Carl Gustav Jung, the pioneering explorer of the collective unconscious, who introduced the idea of mandala to modern psychology. Jung became involved with mandalas through his own inner turmoil. When he first started sketching these he had no idea what he was working with. When he realised that the mandalas that he had drawn illustrated his own inner healing process, he gradually, over a period of years, introduced them to his own patients.

To an experienced practitioner, the mandala can reveal the state of a person's conscious and subconscious mind. Thoughts, experiences and feelings which are too painful to be expressed verbally can be communicated through this form of art. The mandala can gently unlock painful experiences and fears which have been locked away in the unconscious mind and are perhaps manifesting as a physical symptom.

Working with mandalas – creating your own, introducing colour to those already drawn or actively using them in meditation – promotes healing, relaxation, stress reduction and allows one to express innermost feelings.

The mandalas given in this chapter are intended to be used for the purpose of working with colour and contemplation. Select your own colours for each of the mandalas drawn. After you have completed colouring them, each one can be used as an aid for meditation. This can be in two ways. The first is to read the description given with each mandala, then to think about what you have just read while contemplating the mandala and the colours with which you have filled it. The second way is to place the mandala where you can reflect upon it comfortably. Start at the outer circle. This represents where you stand now in time. Slowly allow your gaze to move through the mandala to the centre point, which represents the divine part of you which is eternal. Each time that you work with a mandala in this way, you should receive new insights into what it is saying to you. But, in order for this to happen, practice has to be on a regular basis.

Perhaps, after working with these mandalas, you may be inspired to create your own. In whatever way you choose to work, I hope that you find healing, relaxation, peace and joy.

1 The seven cosmic steps

All of us accept and are familiar with our physical body, the vehicle which allows us to function on this Earth plane, but few people realise that they comprise something beyond the physical, beyond time and space. This mandala speaks of the way in which we can become more aware of this other aspect of ourselves, awake to our own spirituality.

The outer circle of this mandala portrays where we, as humans, stand at this moment in time. The tiny circles contained within the circumference represent our challenges, negative attitudes and

rigidity that we have to work through in order to have greater contact with the eternal part of us, that part which has no beginning and no ending.

Shifting our gaze inside the circle, we meet seven smaller circles encasing a seven-limbed pattern holding a flame at its centre. Seven is one of the sacred numbers; it is the number relating to the universe and represents completeness, totality. In Buddhism, seven is the number of cosmic stages which have to be passed through in order to transcend time and space to reach the divine reality. These are likened to the seven steps said to have been taken by the Buddha.

These seven circles represent the seven steps which we have to take if we wish to realise our own divinity. Each step holds a new challenge, a letting-go of old patterns; a shedding of parts of our density which prevents us from being in touch with that ultimate reality. This frequently is a very difficult thing to do. The old and familiar patterns represent safety and security. To let go of these challenges us to have the courage to flow with the energies of life and also to nurture trust and faith within ourselves.

As we accept and work through these challenges, the dense outer circles disintegrate, allowing the inner flame, which is connected to the centre flame, to grow and shine through us.

Filling the entire inner circle is a seven-pointed star, standing for the seven major chakras, already described in Chapter 4. Seven is comprised of the numbers three and four. Four represents the Earth, the physical body and is aligned to the four lower chakras. Three is related to the soul, the heavenly sphere and the three higher chakras. These seven chakras can also be likened to steps leading to the divine.

Having reached the top step, the crown chakra, we reach the centre of the mandala. Here we find a smaller seven-pointed star encasing a flame of light. The seven points of this star speak of the macrocosm, completeness, totality and perfection. It is at this point that we realise our true, eternal self, and are able to become immersed into the sacred flame of life.

When you have finished contemplating this mandala, sit down for a few moments and think through your own reflections.

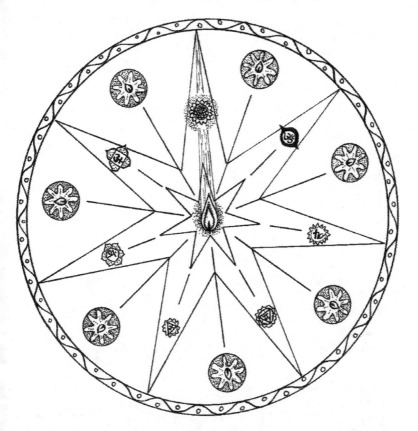

2 BEINGS OF LIGHT

We are beings of light, surrounded and interpenetrated by light. The closer we come to the divine light, the clearer this reality becomes.

Direct your gaze to the stars which form the edge of this mandala. These represent the light, in its numerous vibrational frequencies, and the aura which surrounds and interpenetrates the physical body.

Now direct your gaze to the centre of the circle where you will find the four directions of a cross, enclosed within the three-sided triangle. The totality of these two make seven, the number of completion, of God consciousness.

If we stop and ponder on the triangle, we find there the three-fold nature of the universe; heaven, earth, man; father, mother, child. We can also experience the triad of our own nature; body, mind and spirit. It is this triad with which we have to work in order to grow and move forward into our own creative power.

From this creative power, we move to the equally limbed cross. The cross is a universal symbol from ancient times, and stands for communication between heaven, Earth and eternal life. The number four, formulated from the four limbs of the cross, signifies the Earth, solidarity, wholeness and totality. These four limbs also denote the four elements, four cardinal points, four seasons and four corners of the Earth.

The vertical line of the cross represents the spiritual, intellectual, positive, active and masculine, while the horizontal is earthly, negative, passive and feminine. The cross therefore denotes our androgynous nature, and the point where the horizontal and vertical cross shows the need for spiritual union of these opposites in order that we may become whole.

When we reach this state of wholeness, the universal light radiates out to every part of our being and also to those who are ready to receive.

After contemplating this mandala, spend a few moments in reflection. Try to think over what this mandala has revealed to you.

3 The eighth step

This mandala speaks about reaching the eighth step, the step of enlightenment or God consciousness. This is the final step which all living things are working towards.

Looking at the mandala as a whole, we find that it is composed of an equally limbed cross with a circular centre. A circle symbolises timelessness and spacelessness. It has no beginning, no ending, no above and no below. When a circle is placed at the centre of a cross, it is symbolic of power and majesty.

The cross symbolises the human figure at full stretch. It also stands for the tree of life and the tree of nourishment. We, as human beings, can be likened to that tree of life. Our feet are the roots, which must be firmly rooted to the earth, if we are going to extend our branches to the heavens. The earth provides our physical nourishment and the heavens our spiritual nourishment, both of which are essential for our growth.

In order to gain and have the responsibility of this sacred power, and to achieve the majesty which the cross and circle speak of, we have to learn to master all aspects of our being. The four points of the cross tell us this by teaching us moderation in all things. They tell us that we should not overeat or starve ourselves; neither should

we sleep too much nor too little; to speak only when it is constructive and necessary, and to meditate more so that we may become integrated into the spiritual life.

Shifting our gaze to inside the circle, we find eight smaller circles, each encompassing a four-pointed star. Spiritually, the number eight is the goal of the initiate. Having climbed the seven steps and passed through the seven stages of initiation, the seeker finds himself at the eighth step where he becomes immersed in a cosmic sea of love.

At the centre of this mandala are three concentric circles. These represent the past, present and future which at this stage of development become integrated into the now. All things are now.

The past no longer exists, the future is a dream, which only leaves the present moment, the now.

4 The caduceus

This mandala talks about duality, polarity and how we have to unite and transcend these in order to become whole.

To become whole we have to accept the duality of our nature. We have to accept the masculine and the feminine energies within us. We have to accept the good and the bad, the positive and the negative. To become whole we have to transcend polarity. This brings us to a state of no thing. Rhythm is the basic pattern of all life. Destroy rhythm and we destroy life.

Yoga philosophy has a wonderful way of describing this. It likens polarity to a swinging pendulum, upon which, at various points along its axis, we sit. The pendulum swings to the right, leaving us feeling happy and content, positive, full of energy, etc., only to swing back to the left, leaving us feeling discontented and sad, negative and lifeless. Our lives' journeys present the challenge to travel up the pendulum to its point of fixture. It is here that movement no longer exists; it is at this point that the negative and positive, yin and yang, masculine and feminine become integrated into wholeness.

As you contemplate this mandala, move your awareness to inside the circle. Anything that is worked within a circle is protected. The first objects seen are two birds in flight. These two birds portray our duality; the manifest and the unmanifest; the left and right hemispheres of the brain; darkness and light.

The birds are pointing towards the caduceus, also known as 'the wand' or 'Herald's staff'. This is the symbol adopted by the medical profession. It comprises the wand (the central staff), around which two serpents are entwined. At the top of the staff are two wings.

The staff is symbolic of power and is said to be the 'axis mundi' which all mediator-messenger gods travel between Heaven and Earth.

Mid-way along the staff is the heart, embraced on either side by wings. The heart is the centre of being on both the physical and spiritual planes and represents the central wisdom of feeling, compassion and understanding. When we work towards uniting our dualistic energies, we must do so with compassion, love and understanding of ourselves. This will then enable us to radiate these qualities to all those who we come into contact with.

As we gain mastery over ourselves and work at uniting the dualism of our nature, so we reach the wings at the top of the staff. This point is aligned to the brow chakra. The wings depict victory, the flight of freedom, the sacred power and divinity of the deity. It is only when we have reached this point that we can, through unconditional love, become one with that ultimate reality.

Sit for a few moments in silence and try to comprehend what this mandala says to you. It may speak of something completely different, something which is very right for you at this present moment. You might find it useful to keep a diary to note down your experiences and to gauge your pattern of growth.

5 ꜰʟɪɢʜᴛ

This mandala (see page 84) speaks about the freedom of flight, gained through our work to transcend the physical realm.

At this stage in our development, we have broken down all the old patterns that hindered us in our quest, and have learnt to master our own energies. We have come to realise that this world is transient, it is maya, illusion. The illuminated state which we have now reached brings us that perfect peace and understanding which very few people have experienced.

We are free. Although we still live in a physical body, in the physical world, its problems, anxieties and strife no longer affect us. We are in the world, but not of the world. As Christ said: 'I and my Father are one', inferring that He had realised and become one with the divine consciousness that dwells in each one of us.

It is only now that we, like the birds in this mandala, are able to have freedom of flight; freedom to be who we truly are. When this happens and our duality becomes integrated into the one, it is like a tremendous explosion of light that fills every cell of our being. Now we are ready to allow this light to be channelled through us to those who are ready to receive.

6 ϻaɴ

With this mandala, we start at the centre with the five-pointed star set in the pentagram. Both of these symbols stand for the human

figure with outstretched arms and legs; the human microcosm within the macrocosm of the circle.

The five points of the star and pentagram represent the five senses and the five elements relating to us. The five-pointed star also depicts our integral individuality and integral aspirations.

Around the pentagram lie ten five-pointed stars. Ten is the number of the cosmos. It contains all numbers and therefore all possibilities. Ten is the perfect number, the return to one, to unity.

As you contemplate this mandala, what does it say to you? Are you aware that your whole being constitutes a tiny universe? Are you

aware that all things are possible for you if you really want and work for them? Take a moment to reflect upon your life. Speculate on some of the things that you would really like to achieve, and then visualise yourself doing them. Likewise, own the things that are no longer right for you and work towards eradicating them from your life. This could constitute change which often demands courage and trust. If we summon the courage to walk through the changes necessary, we will find new doors, new beginnings opening for us.

7 The elementals

This mandala depicts the four elements and the elementals that take charge of them.

Many people take these elements for granted, knowing very little, if anything, about the elementals that oversee them. The aim of this mandala is to give food for thought and perhaps help to connect and think about the elements which constitute our own physical body.

The four elements, the passive forces of nature, are Earth, Water, Fire and Air. We contain and are surrounded by a fifth element, Ether. Each of the four elements has its own symbol, colour, attribute and elementals.

Earth is symbolised by a square or cube, bearing the colours of brown, black or yellow. Its quality is solidity and coldness and its guardians are the gnomes.

Water is shown either by undulating lines or by the downward-pointing triangle. The colour attributed to it is either blue or green. It bears the qualities of humidity, fluidity and cohesiveness. The elementals which work with it are the undines.

Air is symbolised by a circle or an arc, and given the colours of blue or the gold of the sun. The properties afforded to it are dryness, light and mobility. The elementals with which it is associated are the sylphs.

Fire is depicted by flames, rays or an upward-pointing triangle. The colours linked with it are red or orange. It has the qualities of heat and movement and is linked with the salamanders.

In this mandala, the Earth element is shown as stones, forming the circumference of the inner circle. The Water is the pond upon which waterlilies, representing Air, float. The Fire element is found in the star.

Sit quietly and contemplate this mandala, watching for any images or thoughts that come to mind. Ask yourself how you feel about the whole concept of what this picture is expressing.

8 PROTECTION

If we look in a dictionary, the definition given for the verb 'to protect' is to shield from danger or injury. The majority of people, when applying this definition to themselves, would relate it purely to the physical body. But this mandala goes beyond the physical and is trying to teach us protection at all levels of our being.

The greater our sensitivity, the more vulnerable we become to psychic attack and to the presence of negative energies. Our vulnerability becomes greater when participating in activities which involve a large number of people. Such events can leave us drained

of all energies. Quite unknowingly, the crowd acts as blotting paper, soaking up the energy of a percentage of the more sensitive people. Those of us who have worked to enhance our sensitivity must remember to protect ourselves at the start of each day.

One of the simplest ways of doing this is to visualise yourself clothed in a blue cloak. This cloak has a hood to cover your head and reaches down to the floor. It is fastened at the front by a long zip. Each morning when you wake, imagine yourself putting on this cloak and fastening it securely. Then imagine yourself surrounded by a golden orb of light and protection. Ask that these images may protect you from any negativity for the next twenty-four hours.

Place the mandala where you are able to look at it without strain. Starting at its centre, you will find four double-pointed crystals laid out in the form of two crosses. The crystals manifest the light of our divine self, which radiates out to all parts of our being. These crystals form the centre of an opened eight-petalled flower. Eight is the number which signifies the resurrection of our true self, once we have passed through the seven steps of initiation. When we reach this eighth step, we open, like the flower, to reveal our spiritual light.

Moving your gaze away from the centre, you will find a circle of leaves surrounding the open flower. If you look carefully at any leaves on a plant and then at the petals of the flower of that plant, you will find that they closely resemble each other. The difference is that the petals have taken on a more glorious form. This new form could be described as metamorphosed leaves. Leaves that have moved on to the next level of evolution. The number of leaves surrounding the open flower is twelve. Twelve is the number which stands for the completion of a cycle that leads to a metamorphosis.

Looking to the outer circle, you will find a spiked web of protection. This protects the delicate flower which has now come into full bloom. It enables it to flourish and to channel the light which flows from its centre. As each one of us reaches the stage that this mandala is depicting, so we also need to protect ourselves from any negative energies that we may come into contact with so that we can, like the flower, radiate our inner light to its full glory.

As you focus on the outer circle of this mandala, visualise yourself clothed in the blue cloak of protection and surround yourself with the golden orb of light.

9 INTEGRATION

Several chapters in this book have mentioned the integration of our duality. This represents the left and right hemispheres of the brain, the male and female energies existing in each human person and the negative and positive energies. We are approaching a very

exciting time in the history of our planet, a time when the Earth and all of her inhabitants are endeavouring to raise their consciousness to the next dimension. In order to do this, each of us has to unite our dualistic nature.

The basic shape which forms this mandala is the Star of David. This is formed by two interlocking tetrahedrons which represent male and female energy. The upper pointed triangle represents the male energy and the inverted triangle the female energy. This sacred geometric form is found around each living person and is in a state of constant movement.

As you contemplate these two forms, think about your own duality. If you are a person who works mainly with your intellect and the left hemisphere of the brain, consider taking up a creative hobby in order to integrate the right hemisphere of the brain. If you work mainly with your creativity, endeavour to integrate this with the intellect. If you have incarnated into a female body, have you ever considered your masculine energy. If not, try thinking about this. The opposite applies if you have incarnated into a male body.

Around the circumference of the tetrahedron are stars of light incorporating either the female downward-pointing triangle or the male upward-pointing triangle. Try to discover which of these energies is strongest within you. If you are female, it does not necessarily mean that the feminine energy is stronger than the masculine.

Finally, shift your gaze to the centre point. It is here that we witness the fusion of energies which create the state of God consciousness. What does this mean to you?

Information given with reference to this mandala may be completely new knowledge to you. If this is so, and you do not understand the principle behind this, do not worry. Think about it and allow your own higher self to reveal its true meaning when you are ready to understand. Remember that when seeds are planted into the sacred darkness of the earth, each one will germinate at exactly the time that is right for it.

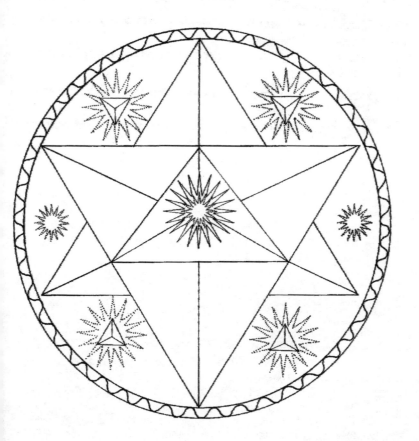

8

COLOUR IN THE HOME AND GARDEN

When you are planning to decorate any part of your home, it is important to familiarise yourself with the attributes of colour and how they blend or clash with each other. The easiest way to do this is through a colour wheel.

PRACTICE

Draw a circle and divide it into twelve segments. Place into three of the segments the primary colours red, blue and yellow (see diagram A). Now add the secondary colours green, orange and violet (diagram B). Remember how secondary colours are produced by mixing together equal quantities of the primaries situated on either side of them? Green is produced by mixing blue and yellow, orange is made from red and yellow, and violet from blue and red.

In the six remaining segments, fill in the tertiary colours (diagram C). These are created from equal parts of a primary and its flanking secondary; red and orange produce red–orange, orange and yellow make gold; yellow and green give lime green; green and blue create turquoise; blue and violet give indigo; and violet and red make magenta.

These twelve colours can be lightened by adding water, or darkened with black.

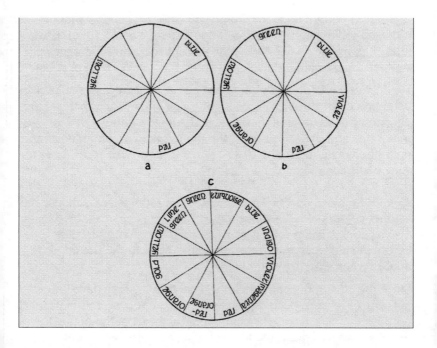

Colour in the home

When planning a colour scheme, it is important to take note of the shade of the colour you have chosen. All pastel shades tend to blend harmoniously, whereas the darker shades do not. Try experimenting with varying shades of the same colour; with harmonising colours taken from adjacent sections of the colour wheel, for example orange and yellow, and with a colour and its complementary colour.

Home decoration should reflect your own personality and nurture your inner needs. Try to evaluate what your home means to you. Is it a place that you retreat to and revitalise yourself? Do you prefer a cluttered or uncluttered appearance? Do you enjoy entertaining or do you prefer to be alone? Do you like a sophisticated or a simple style?

Another important consideration when colour scheming a room is what the room will be used for. If it is a room where you hope to relax, it is not advisable to use the vibrant colours red, orange or yellow. Choose colours displayed at the blue end of the spectrum.

When you have thought about your personal needs and preferences, you need to look at the physical attributes of the room that you are decorating. Take note of its size and shape, the number of windows that it has and their position in the room. Try to ascertain how much natural daylight these afford, also whether or not the room faces the sun. Walls containing windows generally appear darker than those upon which the sun falls. If the room is generally a warm room, then look to the blues, greens and violets. If the room is cold, choose the warmer colours of red, orange and yellow. Remember that red makes a space look smaller than it really is, therefore do not use it in excess in small spaces·or in rooms with low ceilings. The opposite applies when working with blue.

Since the advent of central heating, coal and log fires have, in the majority of houses, been dispensed with. In one way, this is very sad because the hearth was the centre and the heart of the home. It was the place where family, friends and relatives gathered. It was the place to socialise and communicate, and the colours displayed reflected this purpose. Television, although at times serving a useful purpose, is another aspect of modern technology that has helped to destroy this act of fellowship, and with it the art of conversation. Perhaps it would be advantageous to once more create a centre in the home through the medium of colour.

ḣALL AND STAIRS

The first part of the home encountered by visitors and friends is the entrance or hallway. Before decorating this, several factors have to be taken into consideration. These are its size, the amount of light it affords and the impression that you wish to create. This can be one of vitality, peace and tranquillity, modern or conventional.

If your entrance hall is small and poorly lit, choose pastel colours from the cool end of the spectrum. These will give the illusion of

space and light. If using a patterned wallpaper, choose a small rather than a large pattern. A large pattern in a small space can be very overwhelming.

If the hallway is long and narrow, make sure that you supply good, adequate lighting. In this situation, I would use paint rather than a patterned paper. Hanging interesting, unusual paintings along one wall will lead one's gaze to the room at the end of the hallway, as well as dispelling monotony.

If you are decorating the hallway and stairs of a house, and wish to create an atmosphere of peace and tranquillity, try working with Wedgwood blue and white. For the hall floor and stairs, choose a carpet which blends with the paintwork, but do remember that this is the part of the house which will get most traffic. If you choose too light a carpet, you could find yourself constantly having to clean it.

LIVING/SITTING ROOM

The living or sitting room is invariably the part of the home where family, friends and visitors gather. In Victorian times, especially in poorer homes, this room was used only on special occasions and when visitors came. It was kept immaculate, and used to create an impression.

This room is usually the largest, and affords the greatest natural daylight. If its main use is for entertainment, you may wish to create a dramatic, sophisticated effect. This can be achieved by working with the neutral colours. These embrace browns, beiges, whites, creams and greys, and are frequently used to blend in with or offset the various spectral hues. These colours can also accentuate the beauty of a painting, sculpture, a piece of china or glass, or an arrangement of flowers. Neutral colours, as well as reflecting the natural earth, stone, wood and sand, also represent the artificial world of metal, glass and concrete.

Another colour which you might consider for this room is green. This is the colour found abundantly in nature. It is a colour which focuses directly on the retina of the eye and is therefore soothing to

the eyes. All shades of green harmonise with each other. This can be seen in the variable greens of nature which grow alongside each other. In a sitting room, green can be accentuated with pale pink or magenta. Green can also complement certain shades of blue and harmonise with turquoise and pastels.

If, on the other hand, this is a room which you use to relax in, look at the blues. Blue has the ability to provoke spaciousness and calm, peace and tranquillity. In decoration, the diffuse blues are best for large surfaces and the intense blues for smaller spaces or objects. If you choose to have white walls to display works of art, use blue in your upholstery and furnishings.

Eating area

The eating area in a home can be part of the sitting room, kitchen or a room set aside as a dining area. These areas reflect lifestyles in the way in which they are furnished. When planning a colour scheme for this room, remember to take into consideration the colour of any china or glass that you may be using.

When you next eat in a restaurant, take note of its colour scheme. In all probability, you will find that a lot of red is used. This is because red is a colour that can stimulate both the appetite and the conversation, but it is also a colour which is either loved or hated for its vibrance, boldness and loudness. If you dislike it, it would not be advisable to contemplate working with red, but if it is a colour which you are attracted to, start by using it in a small way.

Experiment by applying it in table napkins, candles and flowers, before undertaking the more costly task of utilising it in upholstery and furnishings. Don't forget that included in red are the russet colours and burgundies. If you plan on having dimmed lighting, you will need to offset this with some of the lighter, neutral shades of red.

Bedroom

The bedroom, for most people, is a place to rest and sleep, but it

can also be a sanctuary, a place to be alone, to read, meditate and to rest in silence. A place where you can be you.

The colours which I would choose for this room are the blues and pale lilacs. Both of these colours induce peace and tranquillity, and blue has the ability to wrap you in a cloak of protection while you sleep. A deep blue, verging on indigo, is reputed to aid the remembering of dreams.

The advantage of lilacs is that they generate a feeling of warmth. This is important if the room is potentially cold. Included with the lilacs are the pastel shades of pinks. Pink, one of the more gentle hues of red, can create a very loving, soft, and feminine touch to a bedroom.

If you choose to present the main colour in the decoration, balance this by using a softer shade of the colour or a contrasting colour in the bed linen and duvet cover. Alternatively, if you are a person who likes change, introduce the dominant colour in the bed linen, scatter cushions and drapes. It is much cheaper to change this than to redecorate the room. At one time I used a pale lilac as the main colour in my bedroom. I had the walls painted white, a very pale grey ceiling, a purple carpet and curtains, white frilly bed linen with scatter cushions of contrasting lilacs and pale pinks. The colour of the carpet reflected in the ceiling creating a warm, peaceful atmosphere. I found the overall effect very pleasing.

Study/work room

For studies and work rooms, yellow is an ideal colour. This is the colour nearest to light and is associated with the brightness of the sun. It is also related to the intellect and to mental pursuits.

The bold citrus and metallic yellows add a touch of happiness to a room but should be used only in small quantities in furnishings and fabrics. For large surfaces, a touch of yellow can be added to white paint to create a pale creamy colour. This can take the chill off a room by creating a subtle feeling of warmth.

Using the right shade of yellow in an office or study will offset the heaviness created by any dark, solid equipment and furniture. Another way of toning down the starkness of a strong yellow and bringing in warmth is to introduce, in small quantities, orange. Although orange is less dynamic than red, it is still difficult to use in a room in large quantities. When introduced into a basically yellow room, it can incorporate a feeling of energy and joy.

Kitchen

The kitchen is a place of great activity. In olden times, this was a large room and one of the most important. Meals were prepared and eaten here, and it was a place where family members gathered. It was usually the warmest room in the house.

With the introduction of more efficient and less time-consuming heating, a smaller kitchen was introduced into modern houses. I feel that through this, something very important was lost. Perhaps at a deep subconscious level, other people are also experiencing this and trying to compensate by extending this room.

Yellows have been used in kitchens for a very long time. Perhaps this is due to their sunny disposition. Being the colour nearest to light, yellow gives the impression of cleanliness and of containing antiseptic qualities.

The kitchen is normally a hot room, therefore I feel it would be unwise to use the vibrant colours from the heat end of the spectrum. When we prepare food, our moods and energy levels are projected into the food that we are preparing. Remember that colour affects our moods. A way of testing this for yourself is with yeast. Yeast is a very sensitive organism and responds to the atmosphere around it. When I make bread, if I am in a happy and relaxed mood, the bread rises without difficulty. If I happen to be tired and depressed, the bread takes ages to rise. I have experienced this on more than one occasion. Now, if I am feeling below par, I don't work with yeast.

Another beneficial colour to use for a kitchen is blue, especially if it is a small kitchen. Blue will give the impression of coolness and induce peace and relaxation. This can be complemented with small amounts of orange, in utensils, jars, pots, etc. You will then find that you have created an atmosphere of joyful peace, which should reflect in your culinary creations.

BATHROOM

The bathroom is a place where we go to cleanse ourselves. It is not a place where we spend many hours of the day; this makes it open to experimentation. Again, blue is frequently associated with this room. Maybe the reason lies in blue's association with water and cleanliness. Personally, I find blue too cold for this room.

The biggest items of furniture in this room are the bath, hand basin and sometimes the lavatory. The colour of these will determine your overall colour scheme. If they happen to be white, use neutral colours for any paintwork and for the floor covering. This will enable you to express strong colours in towels, bath mat, curtains, etc.

If your basic decor is neutral, there is no end to the possibilities. Whatever colour you choose, try introducing harmonising shades and splashes of its complementary colour in order to create balance.

If you are drawn towards the cooler colours, try using a blue–turquoise. This colour is made by mixing two-thirds blue with one-third green. A pastel shade of this colour for walls and any tiles will allow you to introduce small amounts of red or magenta to offset it.

If you live in a family home, try to find a space, no matter how small, which is yours to furnish and decorate to meet your own physical, psychological and spiritual needs. The furnishings can be simple. A few crystals reflecting the colours you feel drawn towards; a variety of coloured scarves or ornaments placed around the room; perhaps a painting or two on the walls. As we grow in awareness and sensitivity, our needs, and therefore the colours we feel drawn to, change. If these colours are displayed in simple, inexpensive objects and furnishings, they are easy to change.

PRACTICE

One way of gaining insight into the finished result is to create the room you are planning to decorate in miniature.

For this you will need a shoe box to represent the room. Draw and cut out any windows present. Buy miniature pots of paint in the colours that you are planning to use. Find samples of the wallpaper, curtain material and carpets. If it is the bedroom that you are redesigning, buy a miniature dolls' bed and make the linen to go on it. If you have a daughter with a dolls' house, borrow the furniture from this to deck your 'mock-up' room. After gathering all the materials you need, apply these to your miniature room. This will allow you to see the overall effect of the colours and materials that you have chosen. If these do not blend, it is very easy and inexpensive to change. If you make a mistake with the actual room, it can be very costly to change.

COLOUR IN THE GARDEN

Colour, as well as being used to decorate inside the home, can be extended into a garden, patio or window boxes.

Creating a garden can be very rewarding, but entails a lot of hard work. Once the garden of your choice has been created, it cannot be left to take care of itself. Weeds have a habit of growing at an alarming rate and in the most unexpected places. If these are not dealt with, they will overrun a garden in a very short time. If the garden has a lawn, this has to be cut regularly during the spring and summer months. During a dry summer, the garden has to be watered.

If you are about to create a garden, the best way is to decide the style, layout and what you require by way of plants and equipment. I also feel that it is important for you to invest in a good but simple book on gardening. This should give you the dos and don'ts of gardening; what plants are suited to shade and bright light, and how to maintain a healthy soil. Once you have done this, your ideas can start to develop.

If you are a town dweller, you may have to content yourself with a patio or roof garden or even window boxes. All of these can be very rewarding to create with little of the day-to-day maintenance associated with conventional gardening. They can also offer a wonderful display of living colour.

The form our gardens take and the plants we choose reflect, like interior decoration, our personal preferences and dislikes. This makes each garden very individual, no matter how simple the layout. When creating your garden, take it into consideration as a whole. Try to incorporate colour throughout the year, fragrant flowers and those which can be cut and arranged in the home. If you plan your garden well, it could be a spectrum of colour all year round.

Being aware of how colour works and the effect that it produces on the viewer will help you to achieve the effect that you wish. Pastel shades are gentle and sensitive in nature, therefore they promote a

sense of relaxation. The vibrancy of reds and yellows can create restlessness. Blues interspersed with white reflect a coolness that is ideal for sun-drenched gardens, but a display of very intense colours can heighten the emotions. If you want part of your garden to take on a soft and feminine quality, use a combination of soft blends of pinks and mauves. These could include soft pink poppies, pink tulips and lavender, interspersed with purple and white crocuses. To establish a sense of balance, create some flower beds to display colour and complementary colour.

Low light levels

If the area that you are working with has low light levels, try working with pastel shades of yellow, white or blue. Yellow is the colour nearest to light; white contains all the colours; natural daylight falls at the blue end of the spectrum. Plants in this colour range that you might consider are white hydrangeas, yellow and white roses, tulips, anthemis cupaniana and anemones. To these can be added bluebells, cornflowers and pansies. All of these colours blend well with variegated green foliage.

If the low light area that you are working with is small, experiment with all white flowers. If you do this, be careful in your selection. There are many shades of white and some of these shades do not blend well together unless they are interspersed with light green or silver shrubbery. In bright light, white can be dazzling, but in low light it can take on a magical quality.

Bright and sunny

If the area that you are working with is bright and sunny, use a mixture of flowers that display strong colours. If at the same time you wish to produce a dramatic effect, then use plants that display the colours that lie at the heat end of the spectrum. A single colour will be more dramatic than a mixture. Another situation that warrants the use of strong vibrant colours is when trying to camouflage a dull, uninspiring background, like a brick wall or shed.

For all of these situations, you could try working with bright red begonias, orange Californian poppies, dahlias, and vivid gold and orange African marigolds.

WINDOW BOXES

For those of you who live in a flat or town house with no garden, window boxes can help to extend your interior colour scheme, with the added benefit of bringing life and light to what could be a dull and grey exterior.

The prime consideration with any window box is safety. Always make sure that it is firmly anchored. A shallow watertight tray placed underneath the box will catch any surplus water.

Examples of the types of flowers which can be grown in window boxes include: geraniums, daffodils, tulips, petunias, pansies and fuchsias. For added effect, place trailing plants at the front of the box so that they can tumble over the edges.

Another type of window box which you might consider is a herb box. As well as being delightful to look at, it has the added advantage of producing fresh herbs. Some popular herbs to start with are parsley, rosemary, sage, mint and thyme. Mint and thyme do spread rapidly, therefore it is a good idea to plant these in their own pots imbedded within the box.

Working with plants and the soil, no matter how small the space we have at our disposal, is very therapeutic and mentally relaxing. It teaches us to respect nature and to grow in sensitivity to the vibrant and many varied colours which she produces. It helps us to work with both the spiritual and earth energies. The soil provides the earthing energies and the plants with their variegated hues, the spiritual energies. It helps if we can be consciously aware of this whenever we work with nature.

***

Colour, in all of its many manifestations, will always be with us. Let us learn to love and respect it, learn to listen to what it is saying to us, and allow it to work with and heal all aspects of our being.

fURTHER READING

Birren, Faber, *The Symbolism of Colour*, Citadel Press, 1989

Gimbel, Theo, *The Colour Therapy Workbook*, Element Books, 1993

Gimbel, Theo, *The Book of Colour Healing*, Gaia, 1994

Hunt, Ronald, *The Seven Keys to Colour Healing*, C W Daniel Co Ltd, 1971

Lüscher, Dr Max, *The Lüscher Colour Test*, Pan Books, 1970

Powell, Arthur E, *The Etheric Double*, The Theosophical Publishing House, 1925

Ozaniec, Naomi, *Chakras for Beginners*, Hodder & Stoughton, 1994

Wills, Pauline, *The Reflexology and Colour Therapy Workbook*, Element Books, 1992

Wills, Pauline, *Colour Therapy*, Element Books, 1993

Wilson, Annie and Lilla Bek, *What Colour Are You?*, Turnstone Press Ltd, 1981

Wright, Angela, *The Beginner's Guide to Colour Psychology*, Kyle Cathie Ltd, 1995

Choose a Colour Scheme, Ward Lock, 1988

useful addresses

United Kingdom
Hygeia College of Colour Therapy
Brook House
Avening
Tetbury
GL8 8NS
Tel: 0145 383 2150

Reflexology Integrated with Colour
9 Wyndale Avenue
Kingsbury
London
NW9 9PT
Tel: 0181 204 7672

International Association for
Colour Therapy
137 Hendon Lane
Finchley
London
N3 3PR
Tel: 0181 349 3299

Aura-Soma U.K.
Dev Aura
Little London
Tetford
Nr. Horncastle
Lincolnshire
LN9 6QL
Tel: 01507 533581
Fax: 01507 533412

USA
Aura-Soma USA, Inc.
Trish and Will Hunter
PO Box 1688
Canyon Lake
TX 78130
USA
Tel: (210) 935-2355
Fax: (210) 935-2508

Australia
Aura-Soma Australia Pty Ltd.
10 Cygnet Place
NSW 2234
Australia
Tel: 254 11066
Fax: 254 30240

Canada

The Omega Centre Bookstore
& Conference Centre
29 Yorkville Avenue
Toronto
Ontario
M4W 1L1
Tel: 416-975-9086

New Age Books
9275 Highway 48
Markham
Ontario
L6E 1A1
Tel: 905-294 3771